RICKLES' BOOK

DON RICKLES

with David Ritz

SIMON & SCHUSTER PAPERBACKS

NEW YORK LONDON TORONTO SYDNEY

SIMON & SCHUSTER PAPERBACKS
A Division of Simon & Schuster, Inc.
1230 Avenue of the Americas
New York, NY 10020

SIMON & SCHUSTER PAPERBACKS and colophon are
registered trademarks of Simon & Schuster, Inc.

For information about special discounts for bulk purchases,
please contact Simon & Schuster Special Sales at
1-800-456-6798 or business@simonandschuster.com

Designed by Joseph Rutt

Manufactured in the United States of America

10 9 8 7 6 5 4 3 2 1

The Library of Congress has cataloged the hardcover as follows:
Rickles, Don.
  Rickles' book / Don Rickles with David Ritz.
      p. cm.
  1. Rickles, Don. 2. Actors—United States—Biography. 3. Comedians—
United States—Biography. I. Ritz, David. II. Title.

PN2287.R53A3 2007
792.702'8092—dc22   2006038948

ISBN-13: 978-0-7432-9305-1
ISBN-10:   0-7432-9305-3
ISBN-13: 978-0-7432-9306-8 (pbk)
ISBN-10:   0-7432-9306-1 (pbk)

All photographs from the collection of the author.

FOR MY BARBARA

ACKNOWLEDGMENTS

Thanks from Rickles to:

My wonderful children, Mindy and Larry, my grandsons Ethan and Harrison, and my son-in-law, Ed.

Eliot Weisman, loyal friend and world's best manager. He had to be. He managed Sinatra. Eliot, thanks for being there when I needed you. That's something I'll never forget.

Bill Braunstein, my business manager forever. He inherited the job from his dad, Jerry. Bill keeps our bills straight, and we're grateful.

Tony O, exceptional road manager. Man of quiet authority and great skill. He loves telling everyone that I'm a show-business legend. And I respect him because he never lies.

Joe Mele, my musical conductor, who taught me tempo and was crazy enough to convince me I could sing.

Paul Shefrin, my publicist. He inherited the job from his dad, Gene. Thanks for keeping my name alive all these years.

David Rosenthal, thanks for approaching me and Eliot with this book idea. And thanks for setting up a great relationship between David Ritz and me.

David Ritz, a true partner.

Mel Berger, thanks.

Thanks from Ritz to:

Emperor Don Rickles, David Rosenthal and David Vigliano.

Roberta, Alison, Jessica, Henry, James, Jim, Pops, Charlotte Pearl, Alden, Elizabeth, Esther, my beautiful nieces and nephews. Alan Eisenstock, Harry Weinger, Richard Freed, Richard Cohen.

RICKLES'
BOOK

Two guys meet on the street.

"You read *Rickles' Book*?" asks the first guy.

"What's the title?" asks the second.

"Rickles' Book."

"You told me. But what does he call it?"

"He calls it *Rickles' Book.*"

"Why?"

"He couldn't think of a title—that's why."

We start out in the fifties in Vegas.

It was a different Vegas back then. Men wore suits and ties. Women wore gowns. I was desperate for any kind of female—a dog, a horse, anything.

I hadn't hit it big, but I was getting by. I was single and in heat, and scoring with the girls wasn't my greatest talent. On this particular night, I managed to convince some young lady to join me for dinner. She was no Gina Lollobrigida, but she was alive. If I couldn't score this time, I was ready to put Spider in the rest home. (You can guess who Spider is.)

This young lady was wearing a pink dress covered with dead flowers, but she had a set of lamps on her that could light up highway traffic.

I took her out for dinner, then drinks afterward.

"Can we go to the Sands?" she asked.

"Where else?" I said.

The Sands was swanky, the hottest spot in town. Frank Sinatra was headlining at the Sands. In those days, the place had strolling violinists and hors d'oeuvres in the lounge. We sat in a corner and I ordered champagne. (You can bet it wasn't Dom Perignon.) You could hear the clinking of glasses. You could see this was class. My date could see that Sinatra and his entourage had just arrived and were seated in a roped-off section.

"My God," she said. "There's Frank Sinatra! Do you know him?"

"Do I know him? We're like brothers."

"I don't believe you."

"Wait here, hon," I said, trying to sound suave. "I'll be right back."

I got up and approached Frank's party. He was with Dinah Shore and some other celebrities. His security boys took one look at me and turned to the boss. "It's Rickles," they said.

Frank was hitting his favorite, Jack Daniels, pretty good.

"Bullethead!" said Frank. That was his term of endearment for me. "Bullethead," he repeated, "how you doing?"

"Can I talk to you for a second, Frank?"

"Sure."

I leaned over and whispered, "Frank, I need your help. I'm with this gal and I could impress her big-time if you'd come over and just say, 'Hello, Don.' That's it, Frank. Two words, 'Hello, Don,' and everything will be beautiful."

"For you, Bullethead, I'll do it."

"Gee, thanks, Frank, you're a pal."

I walked back to the table and, filled with confidence, raised my glass of champagne to toast the lady. "You are something special," I told her. "You have real class." I thought she bought it.

Meanwhile, I was praying, God, let this thing happen.

It didn't happen right away. A minute passed. Then five. Then ten. My heart was beating fast. My right leg was vibrating. Finally, Frank got up and made his move. Slowly he walked over to our table.

My date was beaming. I was beaming. Frank was beaming.

"Don," he said. "How the hell are you?"

I took a deep breath, counted off a beat, turned to him and, in my loudest voice, said, "NOT NOW, FRANK— CAN'T YOU SEE I'M WITH SOMEBODY!"

The violins stopped.

The clinking glasses stopped.

Everyone stopped talking.

Everyone stared at us.

Time stopped.

And then, God bless him, Frank fell down laughing.

Two minutes later, two security guards and a couple of Frank's pals came over, picked me up, and carried me over their heads and out of the Sands.

I never saw the gal again.

Frank thought that was a riot, and I went home and made love to my pillow.

The kid from Jackson Heights.

ALL HEART

~~~~~

Jackson Heights, Queens, was no special place, but my dad, Max, was a special guy. Here's the kind of guy he was: If he was your friend and came over to your house and your wife was in a housecoat, he could hug her and you wouldn't think twice. There was nothing distasteful about Max S. Rickles. (I never knew what the "S." stood for, and neither did he.) Everyone loved my dad. The man was all heart.

Best of all, he laughed at my humor.

He was an insurance salesman who provided for my mother and me, the only child. We weren't rich, but we weren't poor. We just were. We lived in a plain apartment like a million other apartments you see in New York City's five boroughs.

Dad had a lighthearted attitude about life. He took it the way it came. He was the guy who taught me all I know about car repairs: Pay someone to do it for you.

We'd be sitting in our tired old Ford, the engine dead as a doornail. Dad would see someone he knew from our building.

"Charlie," he'd say, "here's a couple of bucks. Make the car start."

He also taught me all I know about home repairs.

Here's how that worked:

Mom wants to hang a picture.

Max offers the janitor, the mailman—anyone who's around—a couple of bucks to bang a nail in the wall. No one ever takes the money—they like Max too much—except the janitor, who's mad because he has to live in the basement.

Max Rickles was a giving sort of man, but sometimes giving isn't as simple as it seems. I'll give examples:

We belonged to a little Orthodox synagogue in Jackson Heights, where Dad was an important member. Once he was even president of the congregation. He loved the congregation and fussed over its finances. It was not a wealthy group and the building required maintenance. On the High Holy Days, Dad would escort me and my cousin Allen, who later became a fine doctor, to prime seats near the altar. It turned out to be a land-lease deal. Ten minutes before the start of services, Dad would move us ten rows back. Five minutes later, he'd say, "Okay, guys! Find seats in the back."

It turned out my father was selling tickets to services like a scalper at a ballgame. He was shuffling around the worshipers and moving some of the higher-donation members to better seats. The proceeds went directly to God.

In this same small synagogue, my lighthearted father was the only one who could deal with the weighty matter of death. When everyone was hysterically crying, Dad would quietly take care of everything. He'd line up the limousines and make the cemetery arrangements. The bereaved families loved him. Dad was able to deal with death. It never frightened him or threw him off track.

Speaking of the track, that was Dad's one vice. But it wasn't the kind of vice that did him in. He bet cautiously—two dollars here, two dollars there. He loved the horses. Nothing gave him greater pleasure than winning ten bucks at Belmont.

He also loved many of the customers he sold insurance to. In fact, when they couldn't cover their insurance payments, he'd often do it for them. He wrote their names in his debit book and carried them on his back. When Dad died of a heart attack in 1953, those same customers came to his funeral and put a box next to his grave where they paid off those debits. That's how much they respected my dad.

By sheer coincidence, his grave site in Elmont, New York, faces the finish line at Belmont. How's that for God's help?

GENERAL PATTON

~~~~~~~~

When I was a little kid, being around my mother made me self-conscious. I loved her dearly, but the woman was definitely more commanding in her attitude than most. Etta Rickles had to be the most confident woman in Jackson Heights.

I remember one afternoon when she took me to Radio City Music Hall. As soon as we got on the subway, she announced in her most powerful manner, "We're getting off at Fiftieth Street!" I immediately felt everyone staring at us.

"Mom," I said, "talk softer."

"What softer?" she said in an even stronger voice. "Stop being so self-conscious."

We arrived at Radio City on this particular Sunday to find a line that went around the block. I had started to walk to the end of the line when Mom stopped me.

"Where we going?" I asked.

"Follow me," she answered, taking my hand and marching us to the box office.

"Who is that woman?" I heard someone whisper.

"Is she important?" someone else said.

"I'm Mrs. Rickles," she told the lady in the box office. "And I must see the manager."

"What do you want with the manager?"

"It is urgent business," said Mom, "strictly between me and the manager."

Five minutes later the manager appeared.

"Yes, madam, how can I help you?"

"I'm Mrs. Rickles," she announced, "and one day my son, Don here, will be a fine entertainer." When she said that, I hid further behind her.

"We're loyal patrons of this theater," she continued. "And we've been waiting a very long time and we deserve to be seated now."

Mom wasn't mean about it. Her tone was never abrasive. It was simply strong. She was General Patton giving orders. Your reaction was to obey her. And that's just what the manager did. He personally found us two seats, tenth row center. We watched the Rockettes and then a Ginger Rogers–Fred Astaire movie.

On the way back to Jackson Heights, Mom told me her opinion of the movie, but it seemed to me like she was telling everyone in our subway car.

"It was so glamorous!" she announced. "It was wonderful!"

I wanted to do a magic act and disappear.

Back home, she called her sister, Frieda, to tell her about our adventure. Mom and Aunt Frieda loved each other, but they never stopped arguing. After their conversations, Mom would cry and say, "Why do I argue with my sister when I love her so much?" And the next night the arguing went to level two.

DON THE SCHOLAR

High school studies were always a problem. I couldn't concentrate on the books. The words "You failed" haunted me like a bad dream. One particular test put me in sugar shock: math.

I hated math. During this exam, I was absolutely lost. So I turned myself into a periscope and aimed my lens one aisle over. I focused on the smartest girl in the class. I was so focused I didn't noticed the monitor monitoring me. He gave me a look that would have given anyone a nervous breakdown. In a stern voice, he said, "You, what are you doing?"

"What am I doing? I'm cheating," I said.

Dead silence followed. Some of the kids were proud of me; others felt I needed therapy.

Failure was still my best friend.

Nonetheless, young Don Rickles found a way to keep the applause going. He hung in there, became president of the Dramatic Society, but turned out to be a lousy Julius Caesar.

DON THE LOVER

~~~~~~~

The truth is that I had a hard time getting the girls. That's because most of the girls were afraid of me and my big mouth. God forbid, if they'd let me get to second base, they worried I'd announce it to Congress.

When I was in my twenties, every weekend me and my pals—Sy and my cousin Jerry—would go to a dance at the Forest Hills Social Hall. This was the forties and the big bands were in their hey-day and kids were jitterbugging to Benny Goodman.

When we arrived at the social hall, crowded with maybe two hundred kids, "Sing! Sing! Sing!" was playing over the loudspeakers. A few couples were jitterbugging, but mostly the girls were just standing around. Some were built pretty good. We wanted to strike up a conversation, but this was the awkward age; no one knew what the hell to say. So we took a drink of VO and ginger ale (known today as diabetes). We wandered around the room, trying not to stare at the girls. But Spider was eager. Spider was dying for action.

"Come on, Don," urged one of my pals. "Do something funny. Try to get things going."

I figured, okay, let's go out in a blaze of glory.

So I stood up on a chair and, right in front of the whole social hall, in a booming voice I shouted, "WE'RE LEAVING!"

Everyone stopped what they were doing.

We left the gym. Two girls were so astounded by the announcement that they followed us outside.

That was one for cousin Jerry, one for Sy, and nothing for me and Spider.

The comedy game was not paying off.

But Rickles marched on.

RICKLES WINS THE WAR

～～～

World War II.

I was eighteen and available. My father said, "Enlist in the Navy."

"Why?" I asked.

"Because it's cleaner than the Army. In the Army, you'll be rolling around in mud."

Mud didn't sound good, so I went with Dad's advice. In those days, they gave you a pass to graduate. They called it a war diploma. Good thing, because without a war diploma I'd still be in high school.

Everyone was patriotic. I was patriotic, but I had a plan. I was an entertainer. Didn't matter that the only people I was entertaining were my friends. I'm telling you, I was an entertainer.

With Dad leading the way, I took the subway down to Grand Central Station, where there was a Navy recruiting center at the time.

The doctor took my blood pressure. By the look on his face, I knew something was wrong.

Seaman first class and his dad, Max, March 1943.

"Son," he asked, "you feeling okay?"

"Feeling fine, sir."

He took my blood pressure again. The needle went crazy. I looked at the doctor's expression and figured death was around the corner.

"Lie down, young man," he ordered.

"Yes, sir."

The needle started dancing all over my arm—and there was no music.

"You're staying overnight, son," he said.

No one stayed overnight at the recruiting center—except me.

My father was upset. "Your mother will really be upset," he said. "I'm going home to tell her."

Next morning, the doctor told me I had hypertension. In layman's talk, that meant I was a wreck. But that didn't disqualify me. They must have been shorthanded. Go figure.

"I'm an entertainer," I said to anyone who would listen.

"What kind of entertainer?" the doctor asked.

"Comic. I do impressions. I believe I belong in Special Services."

"No problem, sailor," he said, stamping my papers. Bang! Bang! Bang! I'll never forget that sound.

Next thing I knew, I was on a train with the shades pulled down. The shades were for security reasons but, dummy that I was, I thought we were going to see a movie.

"I'm an entertainer," I told the commanding officer. "Please send me to where I can entertain."

"No problem," he said, stamping my papers with that same Bang! Bang! Bang!

Four hours later, another officer came by with a pad. He asked me if I had special skills.

"Entertaining," I said proudly. "I'm an entertainer."

"No problem." Again with the Bang! Bang! Bang!

Sampson, New York. Boot camp wasn't fun. Who wants to run around a snowy track in your underwear at five in the morning? Husky dogs couldn't take it.

"Put me in Special Services, please," I begged my superiors.

"No problem." Here we go again. Bang! Bang! Bang!

Next thing I knew I was in the Philippines. The Japanese were on the attack.

"You don't understand, sir," I told my commanding officer. "I'm an entertainer. I do impressions."

He looked at me, looked at my papers, picked up the stamp and came down with a Bang! Bang! Bang!

That night I was sitting with a 20-millimeter gun on a PT tender.

This couldn't be Special Services. My papers had been stamped, but the only Bang! Bang! Bang! I was hearing was the sound of planes dropping bombs.

Next day, I was back cracking jokes. There were two Jewish boys aboard—me and, believe it or not, a guy louder than me: Irving.

Every Saturday morning while we were anchored in a harbor somewhere in the Philippines, a leaky old whaleboat came by and took me and Irving to worship with a rabbi on shore. That was fine, except that, with the whole crew watching, Irving kept yelling, "Come on, Rickles, the rabbi is waiting!" I felt like I was in the Exodus from Egypt.

I was blessed with a good friend on my ship, Mike Flora.

He was like a big brother, a first-class petty officer with lots of class. Mike looked out for me. He got me assigned to the bridge as the captain's security. Before that, I was scrubbing the deck.

Now picture me carrying a .45, trying to protect the captain. The .45 was only there to make me look important. If the enemy came close to the captain, I would have abandoned ship quicker than you could say "God bless America" and handed the captain the .45.

One night the skipper and I were standing on the bridge. I got up enough nerve to say, "Sir, I believe I belong in Special Services."

"Not now, son. The Japanese are about to hit us. Put on your helmet and don't make a sound."

I put on my helmet, but my hands were shaking. I was so nervous the helmet fell off and went bouncing down the stairwell, making enough racket to be heard in Tokyo.

"Rickles," the skipper barked, "pull yourself together. How are we supposed to win this war with sailors like you?"

"We'd have a better chance, sir," I said, "with me in Special Services."

DON, SUPER-SALESMAN

~~~~~~~~

With the war over, the country was celebrating like crazy. Everyone was happy. I was happy, but I would have been happier if I could have held a job. Back in my parents' home in Jackson Heights, I had to figure out the next step.

What to do with my life?

"Sell insurance," said my father the insurance salesman. "Get a license and start selling."

I got the license, and Dad got me a job with an insurance company which, for their own protection, shall be nameless. I admired my dad's salesmanship and tried to follow in his footsteps.

After my first sales call, I told Dad all about it.

"How'd you do?" he asked.

"I did great. I was invited into the living room, where the whole family sat in front of me. I gave a strong pitch. I addressed the father. In clear, simple terms, I gave him the many reasons he needed life insurance. If I may say so myself, I was persuasive."

"And what did the father say?" asked Dad.

"He said it sounded good and he'd call me in a month."

"And then what did you say?" Dad wanted to know.

"I said, 'Okay. See you in a month.' "

"Oh no!" said Dad, slapping his forehead.

"What I did wasn't okay?" I asked.

"What you did was the kiss of death. Once you get a customer going, you can't let him off the hook. You gotta close."

"But I opened," I countered. "I opened real good."

"Opening is nothing," Dad stated with absolute authority. "Closing is everything. If you can't close, you can't sell."

I couldn't sell.

I couldn't sell air conditioners on a 98-degree day. When I demonstrated them in a showroom, I pushed the wrong switch and blew the circuit. Result: Customers started dropping from the heat and the manager got me out of there so fast I felt like I had skates on my ass.

I tried selling ladies' cosmetics door-to-door. That didn't pan out because, even though I didn't know what I was doing, I thought I could tell the women how to apply the stuff. Later, I learned that one husband came home, took a look at his wife, and said, "Take off the mask, honey. Halloween's over." Max Factor I wasn't.

My big break came when Dad hooked me up with a man who owned a butcher shop. I had two responsibilities— making deliveries on a bike and mopping the floor. I messed up both.

When the bike chain got stuck in my pants and the bike crashed to the ground, a big dog ran off with the meat. I hope the dog was Jewish, because it was the best kosher flank steak in Jackson Heights. The butcher said, "Okay, maybe you can't make deliveries. But at least you can mop."

I started mopping the floor when there were still customers in the store. Somehow I knocked over the bucket and flooded the place. People started doing the backstroke out the back door.

I couldn't sell magazine subscriptions, I couldn't sell ads in the yellow pages, I couldn't sell ads in the blue pages, I couldn't sell new cars, I couldn't sell old cars, I couldn't afford a car of my own. Bottom line: I couldn't hold a job.

Frustrated, my mother said, "Don, what do you really want to do?"

"I want to be an actor."

"Then go learn how to act."

That didn't seem so unreasonable. My reasoning was this: Since acting is make-believe, maybe I could get myself to believe I could act.

WHAT DO LAUREN BACALL, SPENCER TRACY, KIRK DOUGLAS, GRACE KELLY AND EDWARD G. ROBINSON HAVE TO DO WITH DON RICKLES?

Very little except for one small fact: We all attended the American Academy of Dramatic Arts.

Next question: How the hell did I ever get into the place?

Answer: I have no idea.

You have to audition, but I can't remember what role I read. I had to be pretty good or I wouldn't have gotten in. I had no prestige. I had no pull. And once I graduated, I still had no prestige or pull.

So what did I do when I was in there?

It was the late forties and, as a twenty-two-year-old kid, I didn't have thoughts of playing King Lear. I did have dreams, but they didn't include mopping up floors in a butcher shop. So it came down to acting.

I got good direction at the Academy. The best came from a fine director named Phil Loeb. He didn't get real technical with me. He just said, "Rickles, stop eating up the scenery." By that, he meant I was over the top. When I pulled back, though, he said, "Don't lose that energy."

Maybe I wasn't Loeb's best student, but I wasn't a complete washout. I did some serious roles at the Academy. I made friends with talented guys like Jason Robards and Tom Poston. The fabulous Grace Kelly was also studying at the Academy when I was there. Closest I got to her, though, was picking up the scent of her perfume when she opened her locker.

Anne Bancroft was also in my class. She was brilliant. Anne went right from the Academy to Broadway. I, on the other hand, was standing on Broadway waiting for the light to change.

Jason Robards and I became close. He'd come home with me to feast on my mom's famous chopped liver. Mom feasted on his charm, and he had charm to spare. Although he was a serious actor, Jason also loved comedy. He'd kid around and say, "Let's team up. We'll call ourselves Robards and Rickles." "No," I said, "that billing will never make it. It's gotta be Rickles and Robards." We both laughed, and that was that.

Back in class, we practiced certain exercises focusing on emotions . One day I was a tree and had to explain how it felt for my leaves to fall. On another day, I was a duck looking for water. Then I was a hunter staring at a deer. Then I was the deer staring at a hunter.

To be honest, I really didn't get it. Robards and Poston didn't get it either, but they managed to become good actors. I'm still trying to figure out how the leaves felt.

Don't get me wrong. I loved the Academy. It was great training. It gave me a chance to play the Jimmy Durante part in *The Man Who Came to Dinner*. That's the loudmouth character who disrupts everything and interrupts everyone. That wasn't too difficult for Rickles.

Don Murray was also at the Academy with me. We'd ride the Fifth Avenue bus together. Then he got off and made *Bus Stop* with Marilyn Monroe. John Ericson also rode the bus with me every day from Jackson Heights into Manhattan. Next thing I know, he's starring with Spencer Tracy and Ernest Borgnine in *Bad Day at Black Rock*. And me, I'm still on the bus.

"THANK YOU. NEXT . . ."

~~~~~~~~

The fifties were a new decade and I had a new life. I had graduated from the acclaimed Academy and was ready. I had the right temperament, I had the right training, and all I needed was the right play.

Mr. Roberts was the right play. I knew it in my gut. A wacky comedy about sailors in World War II was right up my alley. I knew the territory. I got the humor. There had to be a part for me.

When I got the chance to audition for playwright Josh Logan, I was nervous but confident. I saw my name in lights. Mom and Dad would come and bring the whole neighborhood to see their son starring in *Mr. Roberts*. After that, Hollywood would call. Like my Academy colleagues, I'd be a runaway success. I'd buy my mother a place on Wilshire Boulevard. I'd buy my father a racehorse. I'd make my mother's dream come true and marry into money.

I felt the audition went well.

Josh Logan felt differently. When he heard me read, he said, "Thank you. Next . . ."

It was back to Jackson Heights and hot split-pea soup in the middle of July with my father.

But hope springs eternal. Hope was renewed when the next call came from José Ferrer, who was directing a big production of *Stalag 17*. Another natural for me. Another play that suited my style. Another opportunity where eating up the scenery was just what the doctor ordered.

Another flat-out rejection.

José Ferrer said, "Thank you. Next . . ."

Every day in a different way, Broadway was telling me no.

Broadway, though, was more than legitimate theaters. It was also the home of talent agents. In those days, Broadway was the Brill Building. And Lindy's, where Milton Berle held court. Strippers, showgirls, comics, jugglers—Broadway was where it all happened.

My friends said I was funny. Dad said so, too. Mom laughed, but she wasn't too sure.

Okay, I wasn't in *Mr. Roberts*. I wasn't in *Stalag 17*. But I was something, wasn't I?

The question remained: What?

MEN IN TRENCH COATS

～～～

Nineteen fifty-one.

The Camel man sign is blowing smoke rings all over Times Square.

Couples are meeting under the clock at the Astor Hotel.

Baseball news lights up the New York Times Building: After the Giants' Bobby Thomson destroys the Dodgers by blasting a ninth-inning homer that wins the pennant, the Yanks are turning the Giants into dwarves in the World Series.

The first-run movie theaters are showing *Captain Horatio Hornblower*, *Francis Goes to the Races* (Francis is a talking mule) and *Bedtime for Bonzo* (starring a monkey and our future governor and President). American culture is at an all-time high.

Meanwhile, all I can see are men in trench coats. If you think they're getting ready for rain, you're wrong. They're comedians. Don't ask me why, but back then every comedian wore a trench coat. That was our costume.

When you didn't work—which was most of the time—you went to McGinnis' roast beef restaurant with a revolving bar and a busload of unemployed actors. I'd sit on a stool waiting for my drink, my food and my agent.

Please God, find me an agent.

After all, I deserved an agent. I had worked hotels in the Adirondacks when I was a teenager. Basically it was the same crowd as the Catskills, customers who never stopped complaining about the food while never missing a meal. My job was social director, which meant running the bingo game. As soon as the first number came up, I'd yell "Bingo!" The older crowd didn't find it funny. But others laughed. I figured I was close to making it.

I figured wrong.

Nonetheless, years later I bought a trench coat. I went to Hanson's Drugstore in Midtown Manhattan where the other trench coats hung out. I listened to the guys trying out lousy material. Me, I didn't even have material. I was Make-It-Up Charlie. Even when I was doing my Jimmy Cagney and Cary Grant, I was Make-It-Up Charlie.

But I was determined. So I fortified myself with a chocolate egg cream and made my way to the Brill Building at 1619 Broadway, home not only of song pluggers and songwriters, but agents as well.

I enter the office of, let's say, agent Mo Lippman. In the reception room I see a dozen other trench coats. All comedians. Everyone seems to be either Jewish, Italian or Irish. We don't look at each other. We're too nervous. On the broken-down coffee table is a two-week-old copy of *Variety*. The place smells of stale cigars.

After an hour of waiting, when I'm finally asked into Mo's office, he's smoking a Tiparillo and talking on the phone. He sounds like a Hungarian waiter who just stepped off the boat. He gets up, looks me over and says, "Come on in, kid, stand with me by the window."

The talk always happens in front of the window.

The window looks down on the honking Midtown traffic.

"Why are we standing by the window?" I ask.

"Don't be a putz," he says. "We're standing by the window so no one can hear the kind of deal I'm offering you. If the others knew, they'd kill me."

"What kind of deal are you offering me?"

"Twenty-five bucks a night. The Top Hat in Jersey. Take it or leave it."

I took it. And found myself playing to a half-empty fish tank.

Turn the page and I'll explain.

JERSEY

~~~~~~~~

The Top Hat had roughly the same energy as the dripping toilet plunger in my dressing room. But the atmosphere was great. The club boss sat ringside in a bathrobe. He couldn't stop wheezing and coughing. He looked like he was about to go any minute, but, believe me, no one was volunteering to give him mouth-to-mouth resuscitation. Making matters worse, a huge tank filled with fish stood close to the stage. Some of the fish looked sicker than the boss.

Keep in mind, I'm a young comic desperately trying to make it. But what are my chances when half the audience is watching goldfish playing hide-and-seek behind coral rock?

Jersey had other beautiful venues:

Ninety-five degrees in Passaic. It's so hot the owner leaves all the doors open. As I greet the audience with "Good evening," a squadron of moths dive-bomb into my mouth.

I'm convinced my next Jersey date will be trouble-free. Passaic looks good. So there I am, going along, singing a song, the audience loving me, when I notice this beautiful girl whose boyfriend resembles a small gorilla. Just looking at him, I know he's connected.

"Is that your wife?" I ask.

He nods yes.

"Geez," I say, "she looks like a moose." The audience sees my take and laughs.

The gorilla stares at me like I stole his banana.

When the show's over, I'm backstage relaxing. In walks Ape Man on the arm of his lovely lady.

"Tell me again," he asks belligerently. "Does she look like a moose?

"It's a joke, " I say. "I swear to God, it's a joke."

"If you really think that's funny," he snaps back, "I'm gonna have to straighten you out." His look convinces me that he's not lying.

I immediately run to the phone and call a friend who's connected to some good people in New York.

Following night, Mr. Charm returns, a different man. Apparently, he got a call.

Without missing a beat, he puts his arm around me and says, "You're right. She's a moose. You crazy bum, I love ya!"

NIGHT TRAIN

~~~~~~~~~

I'm in the backseat of a Plymouth, nestled between two ladies. Their dresses are plain. Their figures need work. Faye and Sue are their real names. But tonight they go by Tantalizing Tanya and Regina the Redheaded Bombshell.

We've all been hired to play a so-called supper club off the highway somewhere in Nowhere, Connecticut. I'm supposed to open the show.

In those days, I didn't drive, so the agent is playing chauffeur. Meanwhile, Faye and Sue are chatting up a storm, talking about intimate experiences as though I'm not even there. They talk about lovemaking like other ladies talk about buying lox at the local deli.

At the club, I do my opening. The only ones listening are two busboys and an off-duty cop. My Jimmy Durante imitation is right on. My Jack Benny is solid. And my rendition of Sophie Tucker's "One of These Days" is a big finish. So why is the audience looking at me like I should be driving a tar truck in Newark?

The only line that gets any response is, "Ladies and gentlemen, it gives me great pleasure to bring you, directly from New York City, the beautiful, wild, sensational bodies of Tantalizing Tanya and Regina the Redheaded Bombshell!"

The bass drum goes boom! and the girls go right into their high-energy bump and grind. They might have looked average in the car, but when the lights hit the runway, they come alive. The explosive music is that famous stripper soundtrack "Night Train." The crowd is theirs. The guys are yelling "Take it off! Take it off!"

Taking their own sweet time, the girls slip into their tease mode. Feathers slowly start falling. They show you a little of this and a little of that. Compared to today, these girls could be librarians, but back then it's hot stuff.

Next thing I know, we're heading back to the city in the car. As I look at these two exotic artistes illuminated by the lights of the road, right before my eyes Tantalizing Tanya and Regina the Redheaded Bombshell turn back into Faye and Sue, plain-looking girls from the neighborhood.

So much for my introduction to romantic show business.

THE SAWDUST TRAIL

~~~~~~~

The Sawdust Trail wasn't in Montana. It wasn't in the wilds of Wyoming or the dusty Texas panhandle. No, the Sawdust Trail was on Broadway, right in the center of the concrete jungle. The Sawdust Trail was a place where they charged no cover and no nothing and the door was always open. I knew that because when it rained, the room was always wet. People outside would stare at me. What's that dummy doing? That poor dummy was me.

Those were the days when I was still less than nobody. I was a chair.

The only reason comics played the Sawdust Trail was because we'd heard that Leo DeLyon, a star back then, got his break there. But I didn't get any breaks at the Sawdust. Fact is, when cigarette butts and debris came blowing in from the street, I pretended it was applause.

Compared to the Sawdust, the Valley Stream Park Inn on Long Island felt like the Copacabana. It was a nightspot where firemen held banquets and hired guys like me. They'd sit at tables of ten and get engrossed in deep conversation.

Sometimes they'd look up and say, "Let's give the kid a hand."

Wait a minute, guys, I'd say to myself, I'm not finished.

And then they'd go back to their conversation like I didn't exist.

None of this did wonders for my self-esteem. Which is why I was fortunate to finally find a manager who cared. God bless Willie Weber. He was a second father.

Willie was right out of Damon Runyon. He talked like a corner man in the heat of a heavyweight bout. He had a right hook you had to love. And I was lucky that he saw me as a contender.

"What do ya mean, is Rickles funny?" he'd say to a club owner. "Would I be talking to ya' if the guy wasn't funny? And believe me, I know funny."

Willie believed in me. He worked his ass off for me, and even though the jobs he got weren't exactly spectacular, they were jobs. He kept me going when someone else would have given up. I tell you how loyal he was.

Willie booked me back in a club in Montreal where I once had a problem. Most of the audience was French-speaking. Sitting ringside was a guy in a checkered shirt, dungarees, big boots and a stunning snow hat.

"Hey, fella," I said, "buy yourself an ax, chop down some trees and ride downriver."

In a heavy French accent, he said, "Monsieur, how would you like a punch in the face?"

I thought that was the end of my career in Montreal.

But Willie wouldn't give up. Months later, Willie calls the club's boss and says, "I got a great kid who tells stories the French crowd will love. Plus, he plays harmonica."

Next thing I know, I'm back on stage in Montreal, harmonica in hand. I can't play a note. And as luck would have it, another woodsman is sitting ringside. Only this guy is bigger.

I tell the audience how much I love the French-Canadian people before taking a humble bow, calmly walking off stage, and throwing myself into a moving taxi headed for the airport.

Having a second dad like Willie took on even greater importance on the night I was playing the Wayne Room in Washington, D.C. That was when everything changed. After that night, my life was never the same again.

MY HERO

In politics, you talk about FDR. In sports, there's Joe Louis and Hank Greenberg. In entertainment, Jack Benny and Milton Berle. These are my heroes, men I admire. These are famous people whose accomplishments history will never forget.

But sometimes your biggest hero of all isn't famous. Sometimes he's only known to his family, his friends and his business associates. Sometimes his accomplishments are modest. Maybe he isn't rich. Maybe he hasn't made a contribution that will change the world. But all that doesn't matter when the hero changes your world.

That's what my dad did. Max Rickles showed me how to make it through tough times and hang in when things didn't seem to be happening.

I wasn't thinking of him when I was playing the Wayne Room. I was thinking of making the audience laugh. As usual, I was opening for strippers. In fact, in those days one of the strippers I worked with was Sally Marr, the mother of Lenny Bruce. Sally was a caring person. Her son Lenny would wind up, by accident, playing a big role in my career—but I'll save that story for later.

Meanwhile, back in the Wayne Room in D.C., my career was sputtering along. A couple of politicians came out to see me. On this particular night, I was feeling good. My juices were flowing. I decided to take a chance and do my Peter Lorre dramatic piece, hoping the audience would eat it up.

I called the routine "The Man with the Glass Head." It was a weird performance where Lorre, believing everyone could see into his glass head, was going to the electric chair.

The lights came down. I did what I did best: pure Rickles, making it up as I went along. I took on Lorre's voice. I grabbed my head and started yelling, "Warden, stop looking into my head! Stop looking into my head!"

The audience was stunned. But after a few seconds, they broke into applause. They couldn't believe I had the courage to try and sell dramatics in a strip club.

To anyone who's interested in how I developed my style, I have an easy answer: I talked to the audience and prayed. I stumbled upon a self-styled theatrical performance. I discovered that my kind of storytelling had nothing to do with canned jokes and written routines. I just let it happen.

It took a while, but I found a distinct sense of sarcasm and humorous exaggeration; I found my own comedic voice—whatever the hell that means.

There was nothing comedic, though, about the voice that greeted me after the show in D.C. I was shocked to see my cousin Jerry Rickles.

"What are you doing here?" I asked.

"I just flew in from New York," he replied. "Can we talk in private?"

We found a couple of chairs and sat down.

"What's wrong, Jerry?"

"Don," he said in an emotional voice, "it's your dad."

I immediately froze up. I didn't want to hear what was coming next.

"Your dad had a heart attack. He was on the street when it happened. They tried to save him, but they couldn't."

Dad was only fifty-five, a strong man in the prime of his life. I thought he'd live another fifty-five years. He'd always be with me and Mom.

My first thought was, I have to be strong for Mom because she's always there for me.

Only later did I learn this detail of Dad's death: By pure chance, it was my cousin Sol, then an intern, who arrived at the scene in an ambulance from Bellevue Hospital to try and resuscitate him. The odds of that were a million to one. Even my dear cousin couldn't bring back his uncle. Dad was gone.

Rabbi Berliant, my father's dear friend, officiated at the funeral. "Max S. Rickles," he said, "is gone, but he'll never leave us. His spirit will always remain."

Bet on it.

"Life goes on," my mother said to me. "You'll get through this, sonny boy. I'll be with you every step of the way."

And imagine, I was the one worrying about Mom!

JUST THE TWO OF US

~~~~~~~

For years we were a trio. Now we were a duo, just me and my mother.

This was strange and new. For so many years, we were rolling along as one happy family. And just like that, a light went out. Now what?

"We're moving to Long Beach out on Long Island," my mom said. And knowing her, there was no voting.

Understandably, with her husband gone, Mom wanted to be close to what family remained. She wanted to be near her sister.

We lived in a basement apartment with a lovely view of the sidewalk. Aunt Frieda, whom I loved, lived right above us. She was a wonderful woman with an especially warm relationship with her pocketbook. She owned the apartment where we stayed, and reduced our rent. (At least a little.)

When it came to my career, Mom became even more encouraging.

"Don't worry, my darling," she'd say. "Keep your chin up. You'll make it."

"When, Mom, when?"

"When" took a while.

I started playing places like the Atlantic Beach Club and the Boulevard in Queens. The crowds were warming up to me. And Mom thought it was helpful to stand in the wings and tell anyone who would listen, "Isn't he fabulous? Isn't he great?"

After the show, she'd go to the boss and say, "Did you see the reception my Don got?"

"Yes, Mrs. Rickles," the owner would say, wanting to appease Mom.

But Mom wanted more. She wouldn't be happy unless the boss gave her a bouquet of roses and told her I was dynamite. But the boss wasn't about to show enthusiasm. He was afraid the agent would call and ask for more money.

So my money remained modest while my style got more aggressive. Some people in the audience loved it; some got scared.

The only thing that got me scared, though, was when the phone stopped ringing. As long as it rang, I knew I was in business. And if Rickles was in business, at least somebody was laughing.

SAILING

~~~~~~~~~

The sea is calm.

The moonlight is bright.

The ship silently sails along.

I look out at the distant shore.

I see the twinkling lights.

I could be sailing into Venice. Or Barcelona. Or maybe Monte Carlo.

Actually, I'm sailing to Staten Island. On a run-down ferryboat.

I got a job at a joint that doesn't even have a name. Just an address that Willie gave me. It's a private party, a wedding, an anniversary, an Italian cookout. Who knows? Who cares?

I look around the ferry and imagine what the Jews, Irish and Italians felt like when they first came over from the Old Country. Confused. Frightened. Excited. Hoping to make some kind of living. All that describes me.

It takes hours to get from Long Island to Staten Island, but I make the trip more than once. I'd do anything to keep from taking a normal job. I just can't handle normal. So the journey continues.

To break the monotony, I day dream that the ferry is a luxury liner. I'm entertaining royalty on the *Ile de France*. The King and Queen are giving me a standing ovation. The foghorn from the ferry destroys my dream.

I get off on Staten Island and find my way to the restaurant where I've been hired to entertain at a party for Tony and Maria Gabazano, who are celebrating their fiftieth wedding anniversary. Everyone's doing the tarantella. Staten Island turns into Naples, Italy.

After a couple of glasses of Chianti, I say, "Hold it, folks. When do we get to do the hora?"

"Relax, Rickles. First the salad, then the spaghetti, then the veal, then the bowl of fruit, and then it's your turn to be funny."

"Gimme a break. Look at the shape this crowd is in. If I dropped my pants and fired a rocket, I wouldn't get their attention."

ELEGANTE

~~~~~~

Brooklyn is a beautiful place. Ask any Brooklynite. Ask me. I'll tell you it's beautiful, and I'm a kid from Jackson Heights who rooted against the Dodgers. See, Brooklyn gave me my first big break. Without Brooklyn, I'd still be entertaining at bar mitzvahs. But come to think of it, it's where I started entertaining at bar mitzvahs. Here's the story.

There was a big upscale club in the heart of Brooklyn on Ocean Parkway called the Elegante. Its owner was Joe Scandore. Joe and the Elegante changed my life.

Joe was an elegantly dressed man with an improbably high-pitched voice and a law degree from Syracuse University. He was a bright guy with a show-biz brain. In addition to having dinner and attending a regular show, you could get married at the Elegante or have any kind of party you wanted. Joe was Italian, but the Elegante, situated in the middle of a Jewish neighborhood, catered to everyone. It was where you went for a classy meal, a special night out, or the best live entertainment on Ocean Parkway.

I clicked at the Elegante. That's where my style came together. And Joe was there to witness the whole thing. Joe liked me so much he bought my contract from Willie Weber and decided to manage me.

Leaving Willie wasn't easy, but he understood. He always wanted the best for me. No hard feelings. Besides, Mom was convinced Joe represented a step up. She was crazy about him, and he treated her like a queen. She loved how he cared for her sonny boy.

Before Joe got me jobs outside the Elegante, he had me working his club so often it became a second home. The schedule was nuts.

It went like this:

Saturday morning I wake up at the crack of dawn in Long Beach, take the Long Island Railroad and two subways to get to Brooklyn.

I'd get to a hotel in downtown Brooklyn, check in, shower and put on the tux. Here comes the knock on the door. It's Rocky, Joe's man. Rocky was a sweetheart.

"Bar mitzvah time," he says. "You're on in an hour."

Rocky runs me over to the Elegante where I grab a bite in the kitchen. After the tap dancer is done tapping, I come on to entertain the bar mitzvah party. Everyone's busy eating lunch.

I begin to sell my stuff.

"Is this your father?" I ask the bar mitzvah boy. "What happened? Did a bus hit him?"

"And this is your mother?" I continue.

He nods yes.

"She's beautiful. What does she see in your father?"

Then I look over the room and say, "I'll be honest, this crowd looks like a real mercy mission. So just give me the kid's gifts and let me go home early."

Right after the show, Rocky takes me back to the hotel. I take off my yarmulke and Rocky says, "Relax, Jew, I'll be back at seven."

I stretch out on the bed and think, Why am I killing myself? The answer's easy: I need the money.

Seven o'clock and Rocky comes knocking at the door. I jump into my tux and he takes me back to the Elegante where I do a show at nine and another at eleven.

By 1 A.M., I'm hanging out at the Elegante bar while Joe, with his smooth-talking style, tries to find me a girl. Usually, I wind up empty-handed, but once in a while when the moon is full and the parking lot deserted, Joe introduces me to a young lady who enjoys my performance and gives me an opportunity to enjoy her in the back of Scandore's big Cadillac.

Then back to the hotel where I sleep for a few hours.

I'm up Sunday morning for a wedding party and two more shows Sunday night.

This is the Elegante lifestyle.

"Are you happy, sonny boy?" Mom asks.

"Happy enough," I say.

"Good," she says, " 'cause we're moving to Miami."

HEY, ROSE, PASS THE SUNTAN LOTION

~~~~~~~~

Mom moved us to Miami Beach, where she shared an apartment on Collins Avenue with her friend from Jackson Heights, Honey Schwartz. Honey was also a widow, a lovely lady who became part of our family.

I had my own small place and adjusted easily. Who couldn't adjust to Florida? In the fifties, Miami Beach was a tropical suburb of New York City. You felt a Jewish atmosphere everywhere you turned: women playing mah-jongg in front of their cabanas; overweight men in bathing suits sitting at bridge tables dealing out their hands in heavy-money card games. At Joe's Stone Crab Restaurant, the crabs were two bucks and lobster a buck-fifty. At Wolfie's Deli at Lincoln Road and Collins Avenue, pastrami, tongue and corned beef piled a mile high on rye with all the pickles and cole slaw you could eat were a quarter a sandwich.

The fancy hotels were the Fontainebleau, the Eden Roc, the Americana and the Diplomat. Headliners were playing them all. At the Latin Quarter, Milton Berle was breaking records. Meanwhile, I was appearing at a small, intimate room called Murray Franklin's, where the audience sat in rocking chairs. That was the gimmick. Your genial host was Murray Franklin, who saw himself as the Ed Sullivan of Miami Beach. I'll always be grateful to Murray for giving me a shot.

I'll also always love Rowan and Martin, because when they were headlining the Americana, they caught my act at Murray's and talked me up all up and down the beach. Dan and Dick became my pals and boosters.

I was working at Murray's when I met a guy named Larry King. Yes, the same Larry King who today interviews prime ministers and presidents. On the air, his personality was powerful; at Wolfie's, he became an eccentric who worried that the pastrami was too thick and the pickles too salty.

Back then, Larry had a radio show from 1 A.M. to 5 A.M. He broadcasted from a houseboat. His listeners were mostly waiters, showgirls and anyone with insomnia. King had me on the air many times to take listeners' phone calls. When the caller talked for more than thirty seconds, I'd say, "Don't be a hockey puck. Get out of my life." And I'd hang up. Larry loved it.

"Wait," King would say, "this next caller is serious. He wants to talk politics."

"Listen, Larry," I'd say, "I have no plans to run this country. So leave me alone with the politics. Tell him to kiss my congress."

And so it went—phone call after phone call, hang-up after hang-up. After hours of laughing it up, we became friends. Still are today.

A sit-down with the Great One, Miami in the fifties.

Word got around Miami that this Rickles guy was pretty funny. A gentleman named Jackie Gleason wanted to see for himself.

There was nothing subtle about Gleason. The night he walked into the club, he picked up a chair and a small table, carried them on stage, and sat down not two feet from me. He poured himself a stiff drink, threw it back and said, "Okay, pal, make the Great One laugh."

I took a deep breath and started ad-libbing like crazy. Jackie slumped in his chair, barely looking up.

"Jackie," I said, "wake up. We need you Irish for parades. Take your table and chair, move to another hotel, fix me up with a June Taylor dancer, and I'll meet you in an hour."

The audience laughed and Gleason chuckled, which, given his condition, was saying a lot. He lifted his glass and said with a smile, "To you, pally."

Miami Beach, fun capital of America, was Jackie Gleason's world; I was just happy to be in it.

THE GREAT SUMMIT

~~~~~~~

I was still putting one foot in front of the other, counting on my loyal manager to keep me going in Miami. Aunt Honey and my mother would come see me wherever I was appearing. They saw I was making progress, but Mom wanted more for her son.

I wasn't at the Great Summit, but I can describe the scene for you. I have an eyewitness who is completely trustworthy. Her name is Etta Rickles.

Unbeknownst to me, the unstoppable Etta Rickles had discovered that Dolly Sinatra, Frank's mother, was staying at the Fontainebleau. Don't ask me how, but Mom made it her business to meet Dolly.

My mother was the easiest person in the world to talk to, and Dolly enjoyed her company. After two or three weeks of these get-togethers, Mom learned that Sinatra was about to play the Fontainebleau.

Two days before Frank's arrival, the Great Etta-Dolly Summit took place. The conference was brief:

"How long will Frank be here?" Etta asked Dolly.

"A couple of weeks," said Dolly.

"Wonderful," said Etta. "It would be great if you could get Frank to go see Don."

Not skipping a beat, Dolly said, "Don't worry, Etta. I'll make sure Frank shows up ."

That was it.

And as a result of the Great Summit, the course of human history was permanently reshaped. Two weeks later, Frank Sinatra walked into Murray Franklin's.

I saw him come in. You couldn't miss him. At first, I didn't believe it, but Etta had really pulled it off. If anyone could get Frank to do anything, it was Dolly.

When I said, "Make yourself comfortable, Frank, hit somebody," I saw his entourage wait to see how he'd react.

He howled.

So they howled.

I acted like I had expected it.

"Frank, believe me, I'm telling you this as a friend: Your voice is gone."

No one in the history of Frank Sinatra had ever talked to the man that way. Especially in public. He had never been the butt of anyone's jokes when he was around to hear them.

It felt good knowing that the man bought my humor. I saw myself as the guy who makes fun of the boss at the office Christmas party but still has his job on Monday morning.

As far as Frank went, I knew he got me. That let me go a step further, and it's how our whole thing got started.

Everyone is sentimental about his or her mother, but

"Make yourself comfortable, Frank. Hit somebody."

Frank and I take the cake. It became the starting point of our long friendship. Frank and I both shared a deep desire to please our moms. In later years, he always told me, "Don, your mom and Dolly were friends. That meant a lot to me. It really did."

PAAR FOR THE COURSE

~~~~~~

When Murray Franklin learned that Jack Paar had taken over the *Tonight* show from Steve Allen and was doing a live broadcast from Miami Beach, he started pitching me.

"You'll love this kid," he told Paar's producer.

"Does he have TV experience?" was the question.

"Sure, he has experience. Steve Allen had him on his show. He was a smash."

Murray was exaggerating, but exaggeration is what show biz is all about.

The truth was that Steve Allen had put me in a skit. In fact, over the years he put me in many skits, but the first one was something of a disaster. It was me and a camel on stage. I forget the joke, but I remember the camel spitting all over me. And, even worse, the camel gave off an aroma that could empty a room. Now back to Paar.

Without telling Jack, the producer had me come out in the middle of his show. He thought the surprise would result in laughs. I'd dress up as a cabdriver and interrupt the proceedings with ad libs.

So far, so good.

I walk on stage with a driver's cap pulled over my ears and a meter in my hands.

"Who are you?" Paar asked.

"Maxie the cabbie."

"What are you doing here?"

"You called for a cab. Well, I'm your cab."

Paar knew it was a bit, but he wasn't buying.

Jack stammered in Paar fashion. "Wh-wh-wh-where are you going with this?"

"Jack," I said, "I'm a friend. Do yourself a favor and look for other work."

Jack turned to his producer and whispered, "Who is this guy? Get him out of here."

The bit went south, and nothing could stop it from going into the dumper.

In the years that followed, Jack and I developed a good relationship, in spite of that warm night in Miami that left us both cold.

ZARDI'S JAZZLAND

The winter sun is warm. Palm trees sway in the breeze. Unemployed actors chat it up at Schwab's on Sunset Boulevard. If you're lucky, you spot George Burns and Gracie Allen shopping for clothes at Bullock's over on Wilshire Boulevard. Oranges are budding in the Valley, birds are chirping in Beverly Hills and the blue sky is smog-free. The fifties in L.A. is a beautiful time.

At the corner of Hollywood and Vine, in the heart of the entertainment district, you can't help but notice Zardi's Jazzland. That's where all the big names play—Ella, Ellington, Basie, and Brubeck.

Will Osborne's big band wasn't exactly the biggest name in jazz, but Will played Zardi's, too, and Joe Scandore, bless his heart, got me on the bill. That was my ticket to California.

Hello, La-La Land.

Hollywood was exciting because you never knew who might show up. Like everyone else, I was looking for stars. Unlike everyone else, I wasn't looking for their autographs; I was looking to rib them.

But if the stars came to Zardi's, they must have come in disguise, because I didn't recognize anyone. It was a jazz-loving crowd. The comic was about as important as the free matchbooks on the table. He was disposable. No matter, I had made it to Hollywood and Hollywood is where dreams come true.

From Zardi's, I went to the Interlude, an upstairs room on the Strip where I continued to look for stars. The closest I got was Richard Burton. He must have gotten there by accident. He had no earthly idea that I was on stage. The guy was in a spaceship headed for the moon.

Downstairs from the Interlude was the big showroom, the Crescendo. That's where Mort Sahl, newspaper in hand, held court. Mort made fun of current politics better than anyone. His hip style was all the rage.

I didn't think of myself as hip, but you couldn't call me square. I was irreverent. Some even said I was unrelenting. But unlike Mort, my audience was still pretty limited.

How was I ever going to break out?

Would cold-blooded Hollywood ever accept this earnest warmhearted young man from Jackson Heights?

Stay tuned.

BRAND-NEW SLATE

〜〜〜

It didn't start out like a big break at all.

Most places in Hollywood would give you at least a closet-sized dressing room. This place had no dressing room and no shower. I'm a shower fanatic. I sweat like crazy; in between shows I have to get clean. But here I could only do that by slipping into an alley where a couple of guys held up towels to protect my modesty while a third guy poured water over my head.

I'm talking about the Slate Brothers, a nightclub on La Cienega Boulevard on the eastern fringe of Beverly Hills.

I got there by a fluke.

Remember I mentioned Sally Marr, the sweet stripper and mother of Lenny Bruce? Well, Lenny, now a budding star, was playing the Slate Brothers when the owners took offense at his language. I don't know the details, but they considered Lenny, who others recognized as brilliant, too offensive for their audience. Now here's the funny part: They hired me, Mr. Good Taste, to replace Lenny Bruce.

"They" were the Slate brothers, actual siblings and former song-and-dance men from the movies, who owned the club and named it after themselves.

There were three Slates—Sid, Jack and Henry.

Henry was the power. He was shot out of a cannon. He was a character straight out of *Guys and Dolls*, a Jewish guy with an Irish face. With the men in the back room, he cursed enough to make Lenny Bruce blush. With the women, he was smooth as silk. Henry liked to drink and loved to laugh. The man took a shine to me from the start.

Like Willie Weber and Joe Scandore, Henry went out of his way to push me on the public. I didn't know that this push would be the big one—the one I'd been waiting for.

Picture it: On Monday, I'm on stage. There's Elizabeth Taylor staring up at me.

"Elizabeth," I say, "you gotta stop calling me. I'm going with someone."

It's Tuesday, and there's Jack Benny.

"Jack, does Burns know you're staying up late?"

Wednesday comes along and here's Judy Garland.

"Judy, find Mickey Rooney. I'll throw straw on the floor, and you guys can do a show here in the barn."

Thursday I get a glimpse of Martha Raye.

"Hi, Martha, close your mouth. You're sucking up the air-conditioning."

The weekends are nuts. Everyone shows up on the weekends.

Jimmy Durante: "Take off your hat, Jimmy. It's not a Jewish holiday."

Gene Kelly: "Enough with the rain. I'll buy you an umbrella."

Red Skelton: "Get your face fixed."

Bob Hope: "Don't worry. I'll get you work at the USO."

Donald O'Connor: "Stop dancing on the walls and try the floor."

Milton Berle: "I didn't recognize you dressed up as a guy."

Clark Gable: "Forget Spencer Tracy. You and I would be great."

Rickles carrying the big stars, Lancaster and Gable,
in Run Silent, Run Deep.

GABLE AND I ARE GREAT

Next thing I know, Henry Slate is driving me to some soundstage in Hollywood. Slate's not my manager, but he's acting like he is. That's fine with me. I'm tense and don't mind the company. Apparently, Robert Wise, a big-time director, wants to audition me for the new Clark Gable movie, *Run Silent, Run Deep*, that costars Burt Lancaster, who's also the producer. They say it's a submarine thriller. As a Navy man, I'm perfect for the role. As an insecure newcomer to Hollywood, I'm a nervous wreck.

We walk into a soundstage the size of an airplane hangar. I'm feeling as big as a Planters peanut. The place is pitch-dark except for a work light in the middle of a stage. This isn't an audition; this is a bad dream.

I might as well be on the moon. I'm holding the script, my hands are shaking and there's barely enough light to see the words. I ask if Mr. Gable is present. Mr. Wise doesn't answer me. All he says is, "Please read the lines."

I'm a seaman on the bridge with the captain. The captain is Gable.

"The boat's in trouble, sir," I say. "Should we fire the guns?"

The captain is supposed to reply, but where's the captain?

Suddenly, out of nowhere, a booming voice bounces off the walls and hits me in the face: "TAKE IT DOWN . . . DIVE, DIVE, DIVE!"

The voice belongs to Clark Gable. I can't believe it. My dialogue disintegrates into "Blah-blah-blah." I look into the darkness but don't see Gable. I just hear his voice. I'm confused and excited. Where the hell is he? I'm completely out of whack. Is Gable really talking to me?

"Did you hear my orders, seaman?" asks the disembodied Gable.

Again, I go into "Blah-blah-blah."

Wise stops me and says, "Take it easy, son. Just look at the script and say your lines."

Somehow I do it. And get back into the rhythm of the dialogue.

Next thing I know, Wise is saying, "Good, Rickles, we want you for this role."

I'm still wondering how all those Blah-blah-blahs got me the part.

Another week passes before I actually meet Gable face-to-face. Before that, Burt Lancaster, a serious man, says to me, "This is a serious movie, Don. You really need to know about submarines. It will help you in your character development if you know the intricate workings of the submarine."

Burt says all this as if we're about to be ordered to our battle stations.

• • •

Meanwhile, Gable is one of the most relaxed movie stars in the history of the business.

"Look," he tells me, "I'm a five o'clock guy."

"What does that mean, Mr. Gable?" I ask.

"It means, kid, that my day ends at five. Regardless. Five is scotch-and-soda time. And then I'm on my way home."

Every day at five, Gable sticks to his guns. Five o'clock comes and he's in the trailer. He enters as a Navy commander and exits as a Brooks Brothers model. Driving off the lot in his Bentley convertible, he waves goodbye as he passes through the security gates.

Because he's a producer of the picture, Lancaster is far more intense and worries about overages.

Back in those days, most of the action isn't done on location but is manufactured right there in the studio, smoke-and-mirror style. One scene involves a series of explosions followed by a deluge of water. The mechanics are tricky and the technical guys work on it all day. They can't quite get it right. Finally, at about five to five, it all comes together—the bombastic explosions and a deluge of water. Gable and I are in the battle scene, the climax of the film. Robert Wise signals action and all hell breaks loose. The special effects are spectacular.

In the midst of this drama, Gable says, "Sorry, boys, Mr. Five O'Clock is done for the day."

And then, with all the grace of a European prince, Gable struts to his trailer.

Lancaster chases after him.

"Clark," says Burt, "we finally got this thing to work. It'll cost a fortune if we dismantle it. We gotta film it now!"

Ever the gentleman, Gable looks at Lancaster sympathetically. "Relax, Burt," he says. "I'll dive with the submarine tomorrow."

My nervous-seaman portrayal turned out to be realistic. I was afraid I'd forget my lines, so I hid them under my pillow in the submarine bunk so I could keep stealing peeks.

The seaman character was scared of getting blown up; I was scared of drawing a blank. It amounted to the same thing.

The movie came out and proved to be a hit. Everyone loved Gable's performance. Lancaster was sensational. Rickles was largely ignored, but I'd made it to the big screen. Big things were happening. I thought that Hollywood was mine.

That's the kind of dummy I was.

SHERLOCK HOLMES HAD WATSON; RICKLES HAD HARRY

~~~~~~

Etta came out to the Coast. She wouldn't have missed it for the world. Her sonny boy had made a movie and was gaining a reputation. My mother wanted to be close to the action and, as always, I was glad to have her strong support.

In spite of having steady work, I shared an apartment with Mom not far from the Slate Brothers club, where I was still performing six nights a week. Our place was so small that we hung a curtain that separated Mom's living quarters from mine. It was tight, but we made do. The only problem involved dating. How do you say, "Mom, I love you very much, but do you mind not coming back till four o' clock in the morning?"

Mom became a regular at the Slate Brothers. She laughed harder than anyone, but when I got offstage, she'd say, "Don, dear, do you have to make fun of people? Why can't you make nice, like Alan King?"

Golfing with Uncle Miltie.

"That's my act, Mom," I'd say. "That's what's getting me over."

"Just go easy with the big stars," she'd advise. "Don't get the big stars upset."

One night, after the last show, I saw Etta talking to the bartender, a handsome black man with natural charm and class. His name was Harry Goins. Harry was one in a million. How many guys would volunteer to shop at Canter's for all the Jewish delicacies Mom loved and then ask if I needed help with my wardrobe? Harry couldn't do enough for us.

One day Mom just came out and said it. "Ask Harry if he'd be willing to work for us. He's a gem. Hire Harry and, if we're lucky, he'll be with us forever."

Etta was right. For the next forty years, Harry Goins was by my side. He was the brother I never had.

When Mom and I got a slightly bigger apartment at the Park Sunset, the always-immaculate, always-well-spoken Harry helped arrange her pool parties. Harry would lay out the food in an artful manner, displaying Etta's chopped liver like it was Beluga caviar.

Meanwhile, Etta rounded up guests. I don't know how she did it, but she got the stars to attend. Everyone from Kirk Douglas to Debbie Reynolds to Jack Carter and the Ritz Brothers would show up. Even Sinatra dropped by. I remember one night when Milton Berle sat in a lounge chair next to Mom.

"I first saw Don in Florida," Milton told Etta. "I said back then that your son had a great style. Mine."

WILD NIGHTS AT THE CASBAH

~~~~~~

He was billed as the "Wildest Show in Vegas." The papers called him the biggest sensation in town. I'm not talking about myself; I'm talking about Louis Prima.

Louie might have been the most successful lounge performer in Vegas history. With singer Keely Smith looking sultry and seductive, with his backup band Sam Butera and the Witnesses blowing their brains out, Louis rocked and rolled every night of the week. He sang, he joked, he carried on with songs like "Just a Gigolo" and "Oh Marie" until the audience was exhausted.

That's when I came out.

I was second banana during Louis Prima's long run at the Casbah, the high-profile lounge at the Sahara Hotel.

Every night I asked myself: How can I follow this guy?

Somehow I managed.

Prima had prime time. He was on at 10 P.M. and off at 11:30. That meant my sets were midnight, 2 A.M. and 5 A.M.

The setup was strange. Right in front of the stage was a pit where the waiters and bartenders walked back and forth serving food and drinks.

I looked down at someone's plate and said, "I don't know how to tell you this, fella, but don't eat the eggs. The board of health just condemned the kitchen."

I spotted a girl working on a guy's ear. "Honey," I said, "stop blowing in his ear. His tie is going up."

I watched a guy taking double shots with beer chasers.

"Hey, buddy, keep that up and you'll think you're a beaver and start eating the bar."

At the 5 A.M. show, if I saw that the lounge was empty, I ran offstage, ran into the casino, stood by one of the crap tables and yelled, "Hold down the noise! I'm trying to do a show in there!" Then I ran back into the Casbah with a new following of fans eager to see what this nut case was screaming about.

Word got back to the hotel boss, Milton Prell, that I was running into the casino and carrying on. "Rickles is a nice kid," he remarked, "but what kind of problems does he have?"

Problems? What problems?

I was in my mid-thirties and thought I was Mr. Casanova. The girls thought otherwise but still wanted to take care of me. I had that kind of personality. I looked like I was always in need. If they could read my mind, I'd be arrested.

As the fifties rolled into the sixties, one fan in particular became a regular. He stood in the corner of the bar and kibitzed. He could afford to do this because he was headlining in the main room.

Meet Johnny Carson.

I met Johnny doing my first appearance on the *Tonight* show in New York. To the outside world, Carson looked like an all-American kid from Nebraska. But believe me, he was no square. He caught on to me immediately. He looked at the notes his producer had provided about me but never stuck to them. Johnny just let me go.

At the Sahara Hotel, Carson would get off work and relax by having a few drinks at the Casbah. He loved zinging me.

"Hey, Rickles," he'd say, "when's Louis Prima coming on?"

"Johnny, do me a favor. Go to the Hilton and light Liberace's candles."

"That's all you got, Rickles? That's your dynamite stuff?"

"Johnny, do what you do best. Sit behind a desk and annoy your guests."

With that, Carson walked the length of the bar, stood in front of me, looked me in the eye and mimicked my every move.

"Rickles," he said, "only a miracle can get you in the main room. And I'll make sure that miracle never happens."

The miracle is that Johnny was the one who made it happen. When he got sick and had to cancel his next date, he recommended me to replace him.

You can imagine my reaction.

I wet my pants.

Burgess Meredith takes Rickles to The Twilight Zone.

"RICKLES DESERVES THE ACADEMY AWARD!"

~~~~~~

That beautiful quote about my role in *The Rat Race*, a movie I did with Tony Curtis and Debbie Reynolds in 1960, does not come from the film critic of the *New York Times*. It doesn't even come from the *New York Post*. It actually comes from Lou Schwartz, a plumber in Cleveland. Decades after the movie came out, he wrote his review in a film chat line on the Internet. I didn't read it myself—I don't even know how to turn on a computer, much less find a chat room—but friends have told me my old movies are getting great reviews in cyberspace. Thank you, Lou.

I played a tough guy in that film, and another bully in an early episode of Rod Serling's *Twilight Zone* with Burgess Meredith.

Was I afraid of being typecast?

I was afraid of not being cast at all, so, like most actors, I grabbed whatever came along. That's how I got to play an army soldier on *Wagon Train*, a hit television series.

Here's the setup: Albert Salmi and I are trail masters. We're supposed to drive an ammunition wagon pulled by four hungry horses down a hill to save an encampment from attacking Indians.

"I'm not a horseman," I tell Ted Post, the director. "I'm a Jew from Jackson Heights. The last horse I saw was pulling a buggy in Central Park."

"We'll have a blind driver sitting behind you," Post assures me. ("Blind driver" means that the man will be off-camera.) "He'll be holding the reins. He'll take charge."

A half-hour later, I see that the blind driver is half-blind. I get the feeling he likes his liquor.

"Don't worry, Don," says Albert, "these TV people know what they're doing."

We're doing all this on the Universal lot that, in those days, included a large section of dirt roads. The road we're riding leads down to one of the main gates of the studio.

Albert and I climb on board. I ride shotgun. Albert takes the fake reins. The blind driver takes the real reins. The man is not in good shape. We could be in serious trouble.

Post says, "Action!"

The horses don't move. The blind driver doesn't move.

"Get those horses going!" yells Post.

The blind driver snaps the reins with the strength of someone unfolding a dinner napkin. The horses still don't move. They're too busy slobbering. A couple of the extras dressed as Indians start whooping it up. The horses couldn't care less.

Finally the Indians start throwing pebbles at the horses.

"Hey," I yell, "don't get 'em mad. You trying to kill us?"

Suddenly the horses take off with a vengeance. They're foaming at the mouth.

Thank God we have the blind driver. But where is he? I look behind me and see that he's taking a nap.

Meanwhile, we're storming down the hill a hundred miles an hour. There's no stopping these horses. The camera crew scatters out of the way.

Albert looks at me, I look at Albert. We don't have a clue of how to stop these crazed animals.

We're fast approaching the Universal gates where the security guards are frantically waving their arms and screaming, "Stop them! Stop the horses!"

"Whoooa!" Albert yells.

"Whoooa!" I yell.

The four mad horses don't understand English. They're breathing like they got asthma. They're racing through the gates and charging down the city street with me and Albert bouncing up and down like balloons, two shmucks in Old West army outfits.

Cars veer out of the way and screech to a halt. Pedestrians scream in fright. Buses slam on their brakes. Finally, the horses get tired and stop in front of a Mobil station.

Me and Albert, grateful that our lives have been spared, let out a sigh of relief.

A big burly cop in a white helmet and aviator sunglasses climbs off his motorcycle and menacingly approaches our wagon.

Looking me dead in the eye, the officer says without a hint of humor, "Okay, who's the wise guy?"

UNTOLD TALES OF SINATRA AND RICKLES AT THE SANDS! PLUS, THE STEAMIEST STORY EVER TOLD!

~~~~~~~

Sinatra was the Sands.

He ran the place.

Those were the days of the Rat Pack in Vegas. I never received an official membership card, but Frank made me feel part of the fun. He invited me to the party.

The party took different forms. All of them, of course, were designed by Frank, master party-planner and prankster.

The pranks were always directed at others. It seems I was a popular target. It was Frank's court. Frank was the king, and we were happy to be court jesters. Sometimes the jesting came when you least expected it.

•   •   •

I'm onstage at the Casbah Lounge at the Sahara Hotel.

By now, I've been playing the lounge a couple of years. I've built up a little reputation. For the first time, they've even slapped on a cover charge. It's only five bucks, but it makes me feel good. I'm no longer free. You have to buy me.

Things are going good.

I'm on stage. I see a fella hugging and squeezing his girl. Looking down at him, I say, "What, are you nuts? Take a look at her!"

I'm ribbing a guy who's big as a beach ball. "Hey buddy, there's a new thing out there. It's called a diet."

Suddenly, I see two state troopers walk on stage.

"Mr. Rickles," says the first trooper. "You'll have to come with us."

The audience is taken aback. They don't know what the hell is happening. Neither do I. Then the crowd starts laughing. Before I know it, I'm led offstage, escorted through the casino and whisked into a sheriff's car. Sirens blaring, we race over to the Sands, where I'm taken to Sinatra's table. Frank is sitting with Dean Martin and a trio of gorgeous gals.

"Anything wrong, Don?" asks Sinatra.

"Not at all, Frank. Who needs a job at the Sahara anyway?"

Sinatra looks up and smiles. "I figured as much."

For a half-hour or so, we have a few drinks and many laughs. This is fine, but I hope I have a job waiting for me. Sinatra keeps the vodka coming, and I don't know how to say, "Frank, I don't want another drink. Can I go now?"

"Relax, Bullethead," Sinatra says. "Have one for the road."

"No thanks, Frank. I gotta go. I gotta start pushing your new album."

I'm still at the Sahara at the Casbah Theater, but my status grows, at least a little.

Frank's in Vegas this weekend, and I'm hoping he'll show up.

The minute I get on stage, my stomach fills with butterflies. I look out at the front row and there's Frank, Dean and Sammy. What a treat!

Before I can say "Good evening," though, they take out newspapers, open them in front of their faces and start to read. I can't see them; they can't see me. The audience howls. And I still haven't said a word.

Finally, I say, "You guys will do anything to keep your names alive."

Down come the papers. The boys are pleased. Their routine is a hit. Up and down the strip, people are talking about nothing else. The Rat Pack racks up another one on Rickles.

A week has passed since the newspaper bit. Frank comes to one of my shows with Dean Martin and his close pal Jilly Rizzo. They take a ringside table; they're ready for Rickles.

I'm a little nervous, but here goes nothing.

"Jilly," I say, "how does it feel walking in front of Frank's car checking for grenades?"

Dean gets up and yells, "Rickles, you're always talking about the Jews. Why don't you talk about the Italians?"

"The Italians are great. How am I going to get a haircut without them?"

Just when I'm about to do a little number on why Frank has lost his voice, in walks a group of hefty guys who give me the distinct feeling they're from Chicago. They don't exactly look like the Boys' Choir.

Before they can sit down, I say, "Hi, guys, make yourself comfortable," and go into my famous machine-gun-fire mime, taking aim right at them: "Rat-tat-tat-tat-tat-tat-tat-tat-tat-tat!"

I don't check to see whether they're laughing. But it doesn't matter because Sinatra is.

"That's it," says Frank. "I'm getting out of here."

"Take it easy, Frank," I shoot back. "I have to listen when you sing."

"Jokes aside, kid, who's your favorite singer?"

"The truth, Frank? Dick Haymes."

Dean makes his way to the stage, swaying as he goes.

"I got something to say," says Dean.

"Great. The pope speaks," I say.

"Don Rickles is the funniest man in show business."

"Thank you, Dean."

"But don't go by me," he adds, "I'm drunk."

The hot spot is the steam room at the Sands. It's Rat Pack central. Every evening at five, Frank calls the troops into the steam room. He gives us each our own personalized robe. Mine has a rhino head on the back. Don't ask why.

Inside the steam, just when we're relaxed, a firecracker

goes off under the marble bench where Sammy or Dean or Peter is sitting. Frank's also a master at giving hotfoots. In the steam room, anything goes.

I feel relatively safe in there because Frank enjoys giving me a hard time in public, not in private. In private, Frank's the most personable guy you'd ever want to know. He loves discussing baseball and boxing.

"Don's a terrific comic," he announces one day when the Pack has been in the steam for a few minutes. Our robes are neatly hung, and we're sitting around discussing matters of state, our bodies covered only by towels.

"Don't you think Don's a terrific comic?" Frank asks Dean.

"You betcha, pally," says Dean.

I get the feeling something's up.

"Don's so funny," says Sinatra, "that it's cruel of us to keep him to ourselves. There are dozens of people sitting out there by the pool who've never heard him. They need his humor. They need our Don right now."

Before I can beg for mercy, Frank and his friendly pack grab my towel and push me out the front door of the steam room. A few feet away is the pool area where a horde of tourists have a bird's-eye view of my naked body.

What can I do?

What can I say?

"I swear, folks, it's only a joke."

Frantically, I pound on the steam room door, begging the boys to let me in. Finally they do. I rush to put on my rhino robe and take a seat on a warm bench in the corner.

I'm safe . . . as long as Sinatra doesn't have other plans for me.

DON IN LOVE

~~~~~~

She was seated behind a desk. She was beautiful, she was polite, she was sweet, she was serious. She was absolutely irresistible. She was a highly efficient and intelligent professional, and she wanted no part of me.

She was the secretary to my movie agent, Jack Gilardi.

I walked in the office and said, "I'd like to see Mr. Gilardi."

She asked, "What is it in regard to?"

"I'm a butcher. I wanna know if he wants porterhouse or sirloin."

She looked back at me without a smile. Her face was gorgeous.

"Being a wise guy," she said, "will not get you in to see Mr. Gilardi."

"Tell him I need to take out his secretary immediately."

"That's hardly his concern."

"But it's my concern, and I don't even know his secretary's name."

"Barbara," she said.

"A beautiful name," I said. "Now can you get me in to see Gilardi?"

"Will you tell me what's it about?"

"Take a guess. Work. With actors, it's always about work."

In this case, though, it turned out to be about Barbara.

I had been dating for years. My specialty was female singers. I loved them. I especially loved it when they sang to me in intimate settings. But in spite of their lovely voices, I always knew these arrangements were temporary.

Barbara was different. I couldn't get her out of my mind.

She was poised, she was smart, she was the picture of elegance, she was everything I wanted in a woman.

"Go out with me," I begged her.

"Go out with a butcher?"

"A butcher, a baker, a candlestick maker. What difference does it make? We need to have dinner together."

"Sorry, the timing isn't right."

When would it be?

I pursued her like crazy. Couldn't stop calling her for a date. Couldn't take no for an answer. Couldn't stop thinking about the beautiful Barbara.

I was getting nowhere fast.

Then one weekend in Vegas, I happened to notice her with a girlfriend, the two of them trying to get into my show at the Sahara. They were standing behind the rope.

"Oh, Don," Barbara said, "can you help us get a table?"

"I'm busy now, sweetheart," I said. "Ask Mr. Gilardi."

She laughed. "I deserve that," she said.

"You deserve only the best," I said before getting her a great table.

Little by little, she gave in to my persistence.

We had our first date. We hit it off pretty good.

We had our second date. We hit it off better.

By our third date, I knew I had a chance.

With Barbara, life would be good. Without her, I was sunk.

DISTINGUISHED ROLES IN DISTINGUISHED FILMS

~~~~~

You don't consider *Bikini Beach* a distinguished work of art?

You don't think *Muscle Beach Party* and *Beach Blanket Bingo* are great American movies?

Personally, I was glad to drag myself up to Malibu and work with Annette Funicello and Frankie Avalon in the hot sand. I'm not saying my dramatic interpretations rivaled Sir Laurence Olivier's, but I did my job.

Listen to the names of the characters I played:

Jack Fanny
Big Drag
Big Drop
Big Bang the Martian

Man, this was class.

If you don't believe me, look at the other actors who played alongside me, everyone from Dorothy Lamour to

Buster Keaton to Morey Amsterdam to Paul Lynde to Buddy Hackett to Linda Evans to Little Stevie Wonder blowing his harmonica on top of some sand dune.

These films weren't exactly *Gone with the Wind*, but they were big box office. Plus, I got a kick out of ribbing Babyface Avalon while he ran up and down the beach like a yo-yo. And for this, believe it or not, he made a bundle.

Back in the sixties, beach flicks were America's last gasp at innocence—before the protesters, the hippies and the whole counterculture thing. Besides, they'd shoot the entire picture in a couple of weeks. Fourteen days from start to finish. Not bad for great art.

I loved the employment and I knew it wasn't a bad idea to keep my face on the big screen. Only one problem: I was working clubs up in Hollywood at the same time. I'd get home at 4, grab an hour's sleep and head out at 5 for a 6 A.M. call at the Malibu Pier. When the cameras started rolling, my eyes started rolling back. I was out of it.

But I did it. I played the schlub who didn't understand the kids. I was the grumpy heavy. I got the laughs.

Other films had me actually working on a soundstage. I did *X: The Man with the X-Ray Eyes* with Ray Milland. Some see it as an early masterpiece from director Roger Corman. I saw it as a way to get to know Milland, an icon from the classic films of the forties and fifties. Milland was a classy guy. Funny thing, though, was how they squirted weird dye in his eyes to get the effect of a man who could see through walls.

Ray was a pro and didn't mind stumbling around in the dark.

Eyeball to eyeball with The Man with the X-Ray Eyes
(Ray Milland).

"They're going to mistake Ray Milland for Ray Charles," I told him.

"Not when I start singing," he said.

Milland, like Gable, was a strict five o'clock man. When the clock hit five, work stopped and recreation began. Ray liked to relax with a little taste and, no matter how much Corman complained, Milland's routine could not be disturbed. This was old-school Hollywood. I loved being a part of it, although my part was pretty damn small.

Meanwhile, back to the beach.

The beach movies were paying my bills, and the bikinis were keeping me interested in the scenery. It was fun to observe the antics of the young. The youth culture was changing. The change seemed to happen almost overnight. And I got a taste of it one night when I was playing the lounge at the Deauville Hotel in Miami Beach.

Ladies and gentlemen . . .

. . . MEET THE BEATLES

~~~~~~

The British have landed.

I'm happy to see them, mainly because the minute John Lennon and George Harrison appear, the lounge at the Deauville fills up. The Beatles are the new sensation, and everyone wants to see them. They take a table off to the side, and the girls start screaming.

But the Beatles aren't staying. They're only here for a quick hello and a few pictures with yours truly. Just like that, they get up and leave. And just like that, the room goes from full to empty, and I'm up there entertaining me.

The culture might have been changing with the Rolling Stones and the Beatles, but the old guard was hanging tough.

Back in Vegas, Judy Garland was starring at the Sahara Congo Room and would occasionally come to see me in the lounge.

Judy loved laughing. She had great spirit, and when she laughed, you felt the whole room shake.

"Judy," I said when I saw her in the audience. "A grown woman skipping down the road with Bert Lahr in a lion's suit isn't exactly normal. And that Tin Man business . . . please, that's really pushing it. I happen to know that Toto the dog has a drug problem. And in case you haven't heard, the Yellow Brick Road is now in a lousy neighborhood. So please just sing 'Over the Rainbow' and we'll all go home early."

Judy loved it but expressed her appreciation in a peculiar way. After the show, she came backstage holding a glass of Liebfraumilch and poured it all over my head. Laughingly, she said, "Don, I baptize you in the name of Mickey Rooney."

The stagehands howled.

I howled.

I smelled of Liebfraumilch so bad a winery wanted to cork me.

A MAGICAL TIME

~~~~~~

It was happening and it was beautiful.

I had proposed, my Barbara had accepted and we were getting married.

Mom and I went with Barbara to Philadelphia to meet Barb's mother, Eleanor Sklar. Mom Sklar was a lovely woman who lived in a beautiful two-story house. We were all sitting on the couch in the living room, making small talk, when their maid walked down the stairs.

"Look at this," my mother whispered in my ear, "they have a maid. They must have money."

Two weeks later, they were borrowing.

Meanwhile, pals wanted to throw me a stag party, and why not?

Red Buttons showed up in drag dressed as my mother. He was brilliant, but scary. I thought he was my mother.

A week later, my cousin Allen and I were at the Lexington Hotel in New York, preparing for the wedding. We didn't fall asleep until 3 A.M. Then at 4, the phone rang.

This was taken on the top of the cake.

It was Cantor Yavneh, from my childhood synagogue in Jackson Heights, who was scheduled to sing at my wedding in a few hours.

"Anything wrong, Cantor?" I asked.

"Everything's fine, Don. I just want you and Allen to get dressed and meet me downstairs in a half-hour."

"Now? At four in the morning?"

"Yes, now. Please."

Rubbing sleep from our eyes, we got downstairs just as the cantor drove up in his old Chrysler. "Get in, boys," he said.

"Where are we going, Cantor?" asked Allen.

"You'll see soon enough," he said.

Silently we drove through the sleeping city until we reached Elmont, Long Island. When I saw the cemetery where my dad was buried, I understood.

We got out of the car. The air was thick with fog. The atmosphere was eerie, chilling. We walked past dozens of graves until we found my dad's. The cantor put on his white robe and prayer shawl. In the still of morning, standing over my dear father's grave, he sang the Hebrew prayer for the dead. He wailed; he sang with such tender feeling and heartfelt anguish that I felt the presence of God Almighty in every fiber of my being. Afterward, we recited the Kaddish, the Jewish mourners' prayer, our words melting the morning fog to tears.

Before we left, the cantor sang a prayer in Hebrew, inviting Dad to my wedding. Then he finished by saying, "May your soul be with us forever."

DAY OF DAYS

~~~~~

Back to Brooklyn.

Back to Ocean Parkway.

Back to the Elegante nightclub.

Back to Joe Scandore, looking sharp and greeting guests at the door.

Back to Rocky helping me on with my tux.

Back to the place filling up with hundreds of people.

Back to the scene of my first real success.

Back to my mom, Etta, beaming with pride.

Back to feeling that everyone's rooting for me, that everyone cares.

Only this time I'm not kidding around.

Barbara and I have just been married in an Orthodox synagogue, Young Israel of Flatbush.

Now we're at the reception, held at the Elegante, where Scandore has done the place over—new carpets, fancy drapes—just to let me know how much he cares. For once in his life, Rickles is speechless.

Jerry and Rita Vale congratulate us. Steve Lawrence and Eydie Gorme get up and start singing, "More than the greatest love the world has known . . ." By the time they get to the second verse, I'm a mess. My tears are flowing; my life has turned to gold. My Barbara will be with me always.

I'm thirty-eight and couldn't be happier.

A few minutes after Stevie and Eydie pour out "More," I'm back to form.

"Stevie and Eydie," I say, "you sang beautifully. But I had no idea you'd ask for money."

KING CARSON

~~~~~~

I'm in the guest chair. Johnny's behind his desk, cigarette in hand.

"I hear you and your mother are close, Don," he says. "How is she?"

"You don't know my mother, Johnny, and you don't care about my mother, so why are you asking about my mother?"

"I see you're in a good mood tonight, Don."

"I am in a good mood. How's your mother, John? Is she still working on your farm?"

"Rickles, so now you're coming out with your A stuff."

"For the money you pay me, Johnny, I can't even buy Ed drinks. Am I right, Ed?"

"Keep me out of this, Rickles," Ed says with his hearty laugh.

"See that, Ed, when I need you, you turn on me. And you, Johnny, you remind me of a squealer in prison."

"Now what does that mean?" Johnny asks.

"Who cares?" I ask. "You hear the audience. They're laughing, aren't they?"

In the sixties, Johnny was on the rise. His great reign as King of Talk had begun. He was still in New York when I first came on his show.

People said that whenever I went on the *Tonight* show, it was an event. Johnny would get off his notes and shoot with both barrels. We had a ball.

We also became friends.

One year he had an idea for his birthday: a scavenger hunt. Leave it to Johnny to hire a dozen limos and drivers, assign three guests to a limo and then send everyone out to hunt down their item somewhere in Manhattan.

I was assigned to find a rag doll in a toy store in the Times Square area. The birthday boy himself was in my limo along with Rosalind Russell. The adventure was on.

I'm riding in the back with Rosalind while Johnny is busy mixing us drinks. Johnny's feeling good.

"You're playing bartender," I tell him, "while I'm here entertaining Auntie Mame."

Rosalind is a wonderful sport. She's having the time of her life. When we arrive at the store, we have a small conference. Who's going into the store to buy the doll?

"We all are!" says Carson. "We're a team."

The team of Carson, Russell and Rickles walks into a store that hasn't seen a cleaning crew since World War II. Johnny and I are in tuxes; Rosalind is in an evening gown. The poor clerk is asleep. He opens his eyes and looks at us. I figure he'll be thrilled to see Johnny Carson and Rosalind Russell. He closes his eyes again. He doesn't know who they are and couldn't care less.

Rosalind finds the doll.

I buy it. Buck and a half.

Happy Birthday, Johnny.

FRIENDS? IMPOSSIBLE!

Like so many other good things in my life, this one happens at the Sahara in Vegas.

I'm playing the lounge, while Bob Newhart, a hot comic from Chicago, is in the main room at the Sands.

"I want you to meet Bob," says Barbara, whose close friend is Bob's wife, Ginnie. Ginnie is a former actress and daughter of Bill Quinn, a prominent character actor. Good people.

"Tell 'em to meet us at the coffee shop after my show," I suggest.

"I'll invite them to the show," says Barbara.

"Great."

"But if they do come," says my wife in her prim and proper way, "go easy on them. These are people you really don't know."

"Fine, Barbara. Don't worry."

Show starts.

I spot a guy in the audience whose taste in clothes makes him look like Emmett Kelly. "Who picks out your wardrobe?" I ask. "Ray Charles?"

"No need to turn on me, Bob."

I ask another guy, who's on the heavy side, "How much do you weigh?"

"About two-fifty," he says.

"On the left side of your ass you weigh two-fifty."

I spot Newhart and Ginnie with Barbara.

"Ladies and gentlemen," I say, "we're honored to have a very talented man in our audience tonight. If you like that type of humor, you definitely have a problem. Tonight he's with his wife, Ginnie, a fabulous hooker from Long Island."

Barbara's face makes a left turn.

After the show, Ginnie, Barbara and Bob are waiting for me in the coffee shop.

"Thanks, dear, for being so kind to my friends," says Barbara.

"Rickles," says Newhart, "you're a different kind of comic. It's not every day someone calls my wife a hooker."

"Bob," I reply, "you heard the laughs. I made Ginnie a star."

"What I can't figure out, Rickles, is how you do what you do and still live."

"It's easy, Bob. I'm a genius."

The kibitzing stops and like normal people we talk about everyday life.

Doesn't matter that we're two guys from two different worlds; doesn't matter that I'm a loudmouth and he's a librarian. The bond between Ginnie and Barbara soon extends to Bob and me.

Turns out we all have the same basic values: nutty humor and family love.

We become lifelong friends, and the two couples—the Rickleses and the Newharts—travel the world together, a comedy act on the road.

More on that later.

Meanwhile, Rickles is slowly but surely moving up.

Welcome to the Copa.

"RICKLES? NOT IN MY PLACE!"

~~~~~~

That's what Jules Podell, boss of the Copacabana, New York's most famous nightclub, used to say about me.

"He's an insult comic," he insisted. "Not my style."

By then I had played Basin Street East, a well-known nightclub, with great success. But the Copa was the ultimate.

Mr. Podell was powerful. He even put his name above the title, calling it "Jules Podell's Copacabana." He ran the place. But, as everyone in show business knew, at that time other important people were involved. As it turned out, those important people liked me. They saw me as a down-to-earth guy. Of course, it didn't hurt that Sinatra was heading my fan club. It took a while, but Podell finally came around and hired me.

Opening night was nuts. There was a blizzard, so I arrived a couple of hours early. Even then the line in front of 10 East 60th Street snaked around the block. You couldn't get near the place.

"I gotta get in," said Vito, a guy well known for his powers of persuasion. Vito was the size of a small truck.

"Sorry," said the doorman. "We're sold out. Both shows."

Vito wouldn't budge, but neither would the doorman. The argument went back and forth until the doorman got fed up and turned away. Next thing you know, steam was rising off the doorman's long coat. Vito had relieved himself on the doorman.

Before the show started, I was invited into the kitchen to have a drink with Mr. Podell. He always sat on a stool next to the cash register. He never failed to have the Chinese cooks gather around me and cheer, "Hip hip hooray for Rickles!" Then Mr. Podell and I would raise our glasses of Courvoisier, he'd toast me and it was down the hatch.

When the Courvoisier kicked in, Rickles was ready to face the enemy.

Opening night was exciting. Tuxes, evening gowns, limos, reporters.

The club was set up like this: the lounge was upstairs and the famous Copa Room below. It was three-deep at the bar, everyone with reservations impatiently waiting for the main show to start while listening to the lounge entertainment, a couple of young kids doing "Danke Schoen." You might have heard of the lead singer: Wayne Newton.

When it was time to head downstairs, Carmine took over. Carmine was a force to be reckoned with. He was Podell's right-hand man who oversaw the seating. Talk about power.

Of course, no one could match Podell's power. With the

place completely packed, he would always find a table for an important patron. Invariably, minutes before show time, you'd see some poor waiter carrying a table over his head with a busboy running behind him. They'd put the table right on stage. Then out would come the tablecloth, the napkins, the silverware and the little lamp.

By the time the announcer introduced me and I fought my way to the stage, the stage was reduced to the size of a dime. If I moved too much, my tux sleeve wound up in some guy's linguini.

Remember Vito, the doorman's dearest friend? Well, while I was on stage, I saw Carmine escorting him to a comfortable booth. Turned out Vito wasn't someone you turn away. Let's just say he wasn't in the toy business.

Everyone was there: Milton Berle, Ed Sullivan, Danny Thomas, Ethel Merman. Wall-to-wall stars.

One by one, I introduced them.

"Ed," I said to Sullivan, "wake up. You're alive."

When I was through with the introductions and ready to pick on a funny-looking couple at a corner table, I heard this voice from the back.

"Don, darling! You forgot an introduction!"

It was Etta Rickles, standing up and waving at me with her napkin. I couldn't believe my mother was interrupting my act.

"Mom, dear, not now," I said, "I'm a little busy."

"I'm sure you're not too busy to introduce our friend Victor Potamkin."

"Mom, give me a break. I'm in the middle of introducing celebrities."

"Don, darling, Victor is a celebrity car dealer."

"Okay, you win. Ladies and gentlemen, Mr. Victor Potamkin, celebrity car dealer."

The audience gave him a standing ovation like he was the Prime Minister of Israel.

Etta Rickles strikes again.

A REALLY, REALLY BIG SHOW

In the sixties, Ed Sullivan was huge. Everyone read his column and watched him on TV.

Ed had seen me on Carson and wanted me on his show.

"Only problem, Ed," I said, "is I don't do stand-up. I pick on people in the audience, and your show doesn't lend itself to that."

"Talk to my son-in-law Bob Precht," said Ed. "He produces the show. Bob will come up with something."

Next thing I know, I'm in Bob's office. Nice guy, creative guy.

"Don," he says. "I want you on the show when we do it in Vegas. Do you have any ideas?"

"Maybe I could come out in between acts," I suggest, "and do a running gag. For instance, while Ed is announcing the Brasini Monkeys, I'll say, 'Ed, the monkeys could be trouble, especially if they're not wearing diapers.' Then when he's about to introduce Gina Lollobrigida, I could run out again and say, 'Ed, this gal's gorgeous, but with her accent and your personality it could turn into a bad movie in Naples.' Get the idea, Bob? I'll run out four or five times. I'll wing it."

Bob buys it.

Showtime in Vegas.

Ed's on stage.

In his inimitably nasal voice, Ed says, "Ladies and gentlemen, tonight we have a big show. A really, really big show. All the way from Mammacutto, Italy, the famous Brasini Monkeys."

I run out on stage.

"Don Rickles," says Ed. "What are you doing here?"

"I think you're making a big mistake with those monkeys, Ed. The lead monkey is William Morris' hottest client and is demanding more money."

For some reason—don't ask me why—Ed changes the topic and starts talking about elephants.

I whisper to Ed, "Stop ad-libbing and bring out the monkeys."

"Don," he says, "do me a favor. Go home."

Ed's line goes nowhere. And me, I'm standing there like I'm waiting for the bus. So I give it the show-biz smile and head for cover.

When Ed introduces Gina, I try again. I go back out and say, "Ed, forget Gina. Immigration is going to pick her up any minute now."

In the famous Sullivan manner, he says, "Rickles, I'm telling Immigration where you are."

The audience doesn't get it, and neither do I. Sullivan has no idea what's going on, and I wasn't about to tell him.

When the show's over, Ed comes up to me and says, "We were dynamite together, weren't we, Don?"

Ed still doesn't have a clue that I fell on my ass, but that's okay with me.

I was on with the great Ed Sullivan.

WORLD'S BEST SPORT

~~~~~~

Barbara Rickles.

Without doubt, my Barbara is the world's best sport.

I say that because even though she quickly became a character in my routines, she never complained.

"You weren't married a month," Alan King once told me, "and you're up there making fun of your new bride. How in the world does she handle that?"

"Like a pro," I told Alan. "She understands me."

Barbara didn't blink when I told audiences in New York, Miami and Vegas about me swinging from the chandelier during our wedding night. I made up all sorts of crazy nonsense. I was Tarzan, she was Jane. I'd say, "When we get home from a dinner party, she takes off her diamond ring, stands by the window and signals ships—and there's no water in sight." I'd talk about her like she was a shopaholic. If I could get a laugh out of painting her as a spoiled princess, I did it.

Of course, none of that was true.

You'd think that Barbara—dignified, poised, refined Barbara—would give me a hard time. You'd think she'd say, "Don, enough already with the wife who can't get enough diamonds." You'd think she'd protest about the sex jokes.

I'd tell the audience, "In the privacy of our bedroom, I say to Barbara, 'I'm a barge going up the Mississippi and you're the dock.' Or I say, 'Barbara, I'll tie you to the couch. You'll be a wagon train going west and I'll be Geronimo ready to attack.' "

For all my craziness, Barb never finds fault. (Well, maybe sometimes.)

My Barbara is also capable of keeping her cool.

For instance: On our second wedding anniversary, Sinatra hosts a dinner party for us at the Flamingo Hotel after my show the Sahara. At ten o'clock, in walks the man. Talk about generating excitement! "You look lovely, Barbara," he says charmingly.

Sinatra orders drinks. Sinatra orders appetizers. Sinatra has no patience for slow service. He tips like a king, but when he's eating at your restaurant, you better be on your toes.

The conversation is light and polite: Frank is talking to Barbara and me about what's happening in Vegas. The hors d'oeuvres are hot. The Jack Daniels on the rocks is cold. Beautiful evening.

A magnificent Chinese dinner is served. Frank starts in on rice and chicken followed by shrimp and spareribs. Everything's mellow, even though the slow service is getting on Frank's nerves.

One of the waiters accidentally drops noodles on Frank's pants. That does it. Accidentally or not, no one would dare drop noodles on Frank's pants. Without warning, Frank gets steamed, gets up and turns over the table. All of China falls on us as Frank storms out.

There Barbara and I sit, covered in won tons and rice.

Without missing a beat, Barbara points to the glass of vodka that she's holding in her hand. "Waiter," she says, "could I have some more ice?"

I can't believe it. I'm married to a Valium.

Next day Frank sends an apology to Barbara.

I say, "Hey, why is he apologizing to you and not me?"

"Because he's a gentleman," says Barbara, "that's why."

DIARY OF A MAD ACTOR

~~~

Maybe "mad" isn't the right word.

Maybe "frustrated" is better.

It wasn't that I wasn't getting work. I was.

I did *Gomer Pyle*, *Gilligan's Island*, *The Munsters*, *Burke's Law*, *Get Smart*, *Hennesey*, *The Dick Van Dyke Show*, *The Addams Family*. There was hardly a sixties sitcom I didn't do.

When I did a scene with Don Knotts on *The Andy Griffith Show*, it became a problem. Don's famous shakes cracked me up. Even though film was rolling, I couldn't do my lines. I was laughing too hard.

"Look, Don," I said, "I'm going over to the corner to think about deadly diseases for a while."

The deadly diseases did their job. I was able to get through it.

I had a starring role on *The Lucy Show*. I played a boxer, and Lucille Ball, a comic genius, actually sparred with me in the ring. Lucy knocked me out.

I missed out on several juicy dramatic parts that I sought—that was the source of my frustration—but I didn't complain because work is work and I was working.

Even the little parts I appreciated. Anything was better than having to take a real job.

I was cast in the TV version of *The Thin Man* with Peter Lawford. You remember the original with William Powell, Myrna Loy and Asta, their beloved wirehaired terrier.

Well, in this scene I'm a cabdriver who comes into Peter's apartment, faints and then just lies on the floor while Asta pulls the wallet out of my pocket.

Sounds easy.

But when Asta shows up, he looks angry, mean and hungry. I'm also wondering why his trainer is wearing leggings, gloves and a mask.

"Sure he's eaten?" I ask the trainer.

"Yes."

"Sure he's trained?"

"Yes," says the guy. "All you have to do while you're on the floor is squeeze this little ball. It makes a sound only Asta hears. That'll signal him to come over. Then, with his mouth, he'll remove your wallet from your back pocket."

"Action!" orders the director.

I enter, I faint, I squeeze the ball.

Asta goes nuts. He races over and attacks my leg like I'm Alpo.

"This has never happened before," says the trainer.

"Let's go again," says the director.

"This time there won't be any mistakes," promises the trainer.

"You don't happen to have a gentler Asta, do you?" I ask.

"The dog's been trained perfectly," says the trainer.

"I saw that," I say.

"Action!"

Enter, faint, squeeze ball.

Again, Asta charges me like he's got rabies. It's worse than the first time. The dog's growling and biting and tearing into my coat.

"The adorable dog must not like you, Don," says Lawford.

"The adorable dog is a cold-blooded killer," I say.

"Let's shoot the scene one more time," says the director.

"Over my dead body," I say.

"If you insist," says Lawford, checking his watch, "but hurry up, I have to meet Frank."

I insist that they give the hound a doggie biscuit to calm him down.

He eats, we shoot and finally the animal figures out that his job is to go for my wallet, not my throat.

Further dramatic challenges:

I get a good part. This one's with the brilliant Ben Gazzara on the TV show *Run for Your Life*.

If I'm remembering right, I play an entertainer who committed some horrible rape. Don't ask me why, but every time a comedian is cast in a serious role, he's either murdering his father with an ice pick or strangling his sister.

Anyway, in this episode, I'm on my way to jail. Ben, a compassionate lawyer, is my last hope. I have to convince him to take my case.

It happens outdoors, so we're set up on a street on the Universal lot. The shoot's in the afternoon, so all that morning I'm working over the lines, getting myself psyched. Ben's doing the same. We're concentrating like crazy. This is a big scene and we're committed to nailing it.

Our initial take is going great.

I'm deep into the emotions, spitting out my lines like Cagney. Ben's terrific, giving me so much to play off. We're deep into it when, out of the blue, we hear this voice booming out of a megaphone.

"ON THE RIGHT YOU'LL SEE BEN GAZZARA, WELL-KNOWN ACTOR, DOING A DRAMATIC SCENE FOR THE TV SERIES *RUN FOR YOUR LIFE*."

It's a tram filled with Universal Studio tourists and their eager-beaver guide.

"Get that goddamn tour bus out of here!" screams Ben. "And shoot the driver!"

The guide is speechless, the tourists speechless.

Problem is, when we finally get back to work, I'm speechless. The mood's broken, I've forgotten my lines, and when I finally remember them, Ben and I aren't connecting the way we were.

My Emmy won't be arriving anytime soon.

MOON OVER HARRY

~~~~~

I told you how I met the wonderful Harry Goins when he was tending bar back at the Slate Brothers. In his own way, Harry was as meticulous and squeaky-clean as me. I'm a two-shower-a-day man who can't stand mess or anything out of place. Harry was the same. He understood my rage for order.

As the sixties progressed, it seemed like the whole country was in a rage. Protests. Vietnam. Riots. Unlike other comics, I'm not much on political satire. It's not that I don't read the papers. I do. I read the ball scores. But I'm aware of what's going on. In the sixties, you had to be.

The country felt like it was tearing itself apart. Racial tensions were especially high. Race riots were breaking out in the big cities. It wasn't an especially humorous time, but no matter what the political circumstances, people like to laugh. People need to laugh. And I need to make a living. So I was out there, playing the clubs and doing my best. Harry was out there with me, and one night at the Eden Roc in Miami Beach, he found himself part of my act. Here's what happened.

From the wings, Harry saw I was working hard, sweating like crazy and in need of another glass of water. So he brought it to me. Harry was a dignified and shy guy who didn't like the spotlight. The minute he hands me the water, he takes off.

"Wait a minute, Harry," I stop him. "I want to introduce you."

He's embarrassed.

"Ladies and gentlemen," I say, "this is my dear friend Harry Goins. How many years have we been together, Harry?"

"Too many to count," he says.

"And you can see, Harry is a black man, and I'm a white man. We obviously come from different backgrounds, but we stand together on this stage as brothers. And as a brother, I must say these race riots are terrible. It's awful how stores are being looted. The burning, the rioting, the stealing. But if, God forbid, it does happen again—and I pray it doesn't— all I can say is, 'Harry, I could use a couch and a couple of end tables.' "

I put my arm around Harry and tell the audience, "I'm kidding, of course. Harry is a loyal friend and there's nothing like loyalty. He was there for me in the beginning when I had nothing, and now that I have money and success, Harry, I don't need you anymore."

Some years later, I took the family to the same Eden Roc. By then our two beautiful babies were born—the oldest, our daughter, Mindy, and our son, Larry. Morris Landsburg, who owned the hotel, didn't pay much, but he gave us a suite, meals, a cabana, beach towels, suntan lotion and threw in a free locker.

I always made my show entrance from the back of the room. Morris liked standing next to me as I waited for my musical cue.

We're standing there when I see a little smoke coming out of the side door.

"You see that smoke?" I ask Morris.

"No."

"You smell something burning?"

"Nothing's burning," Morris insists.

The smoke gets thicker and the smell gets stronger.

"Don't worry," says Morris. "We're looking into it."

All of a sudden, here come four firemen wearing oxygen masks. They're dragging huge hoses through the lobby. Bringing up the rear is another fireman with an oxygen tank.

"Just a little grease fire in the kitchen," Morris assures me.

As he says that, the lobby's getting darker and the smoke's getting thicker.

"Everything's under control, Don," Morris assures me.

Now people are running out of the showroom with handkerchiefs over their faces. They're coughing like crazy. Meanwhile, waiters are chasing them, screaming, "You didn't pay your check! You didn't sign for your check!"

"There goes my salary," I say.

Meanwhile, I'm thinking of the wife and kids up on the top floor.

"Let's go!" I tell Harry Goins.

The elevators are down, so Harry and I head for the stairs. We climb all the way up, get Barb and the kids out of the room and climb all the way down.

The fire's extinguished, no one's hurt, but poor Morris, God rest his soul, spends all night trying to figure out who ran out without paying.

HOLLYWOOD GOES YUGOSLAVIA

~~~~~~~

As the sixties wound down, I wound up in Yugoslavia, where I worked on *Kelly's Heroes*, a big-budget caper comedy set during World War II with Clint Eastwood, Telly Savalas, Carroll O'Connor and Donald Sutherland.

The real star on the set turned out to be my man Harry Goins. If you think he did good in Miami, wait till you hear what he did in the Balkans.

Harry wound up dancing with more gorgeous Yugoslavian beauties than all the picture's stars put together. He was the first black gentleman these ladies had ever seen. Harry told them he was a genuine Native American Indian. That got them even more intrigued. He became the black Arthur Murray of Eastern Europe.

They told me the shoot would take three weeks. It took six months. I also had a problem with the food. Everything was swimming in oil. Some of us became track stars as we broke the sound barrier to the bathroom.

Bottom line, though, was that the cast and I became buddies.

"You'd be great, Clint," I told Eastwood, "if you'd ever learned to talk normal and stop whispering."

Clint gave me that Eastwood look and whispered something I couldn't understand.

Telly was terrific. He was Mr. Charisma. The guy walks in a restaurant and everyone turns around and claps. Right away he starts in with "Bring on the food. Where's the wine? Where are the women?"

When Savalas talked like that, we called it "A Touch of Telly." During the shoot, we went to Greece, where the ladies couldn't get enough of him. Especially when he started throwing plates, as was the custom, at the feet of gorgeous dancing women. When I threw the plates, the waiter gave me a bill for two hundred dollars' worth of broken merchandise.

"Telly," I told him, "the girls' feet are bleeding."

"Don't worry about it, Rickles. To them it's a good night's work."

Telly reminded me of my pal Tony Quinn. Whatever country Telly and Tony traveled to, people assumed they were native-born. In Greece, they were Greeks. In Italy, they were Italians. In Mexico, Mexicans.

I once visited Tony in Rome. He lived in a villa with a church on the property. I wondered if that was a gift from the Vatican for playing the pope in a movie.

"What's Zorba doing in Italy?" I asked him.

"Zorba is international," he said. "Zorba belongs to the world."

I loved hanging out with Tony. He'd encourage me to down glass after glass of grappa. It was like drinking gasoline right off the truck. I felt like if you'd lit a match, I was dead.

Zorba, Ricardo and Rickles.

As the grappa took hold of Quinn, he started planning our careers.

"Don," he told me, "you and our pal Ricardo Montalban are going to be in my next picture. You're playing Irving and he's playing Al."

Excited, I called up Ricardo, whom I adore, and said, "Tony's putting us in his next movie. You're Irving and I'm Al."

It wasn't to be, but next time I saw Quinn, he hadn't backed down.

"Don" he said, "I'm about to do a new movie. I promise you, my friend, you're playing Irving and Ricardo is Al."

For years, Tony couldn't say hello to me or Ricardo without offering us parts. He meant well, but we finally understood it wasn't happening. At the same time, being in the company of Zorba was reward enough.

Meanwhile, back in Yugoslavia, Brian Hutton, director of *Kelly's Heroes*, had hired half the Yugoslavian army as extras. The story revolved around GIs looking to steal gold bullion hoarded by Nazis. Complicated plot. Complicated production. Lots of explosions.

"With all these pellets going off," I told the special effects man, "I'm a little worried."

"Not to worry, Don," he reassured me. "These pellets will never touch you."

Next time I played a scene, crawling on my stomach under fire, a pellet shot right into my leg.

"I'm bleeding," I told the effects man.

"Impossible," he said.

Months later, after the film was finished, I had an operation in L.A. to remove the impossible pellet from my leg.

Before that, though, Hutton had us running around like headless chickens. Hutton was such an in-control director, you had the feeling that Marshal Tito, the Yugoslavian dictator, was working for him. I thought I spotted Tito at the barbecue spit basting a pig.

Another Hutton gofer had the vital job of bringing everyone hot coffee. His name was John Landis. Later when Landis became a big director and cast me in his vampire comedy, *Innocent Blood*, I kept yelling at him, "More hot coffee, John, more hot coffee!"

When the movie was over, I came home and waited for the premiere. The film opened to big business. Maybe this would do wonders for my acting career.

Didn't exactly happen that way. My next role was in a film called *The Love Machine*.

Blink and you'd miss me.

The seventies were off to a roaring start.

Two overpriced nurses—Telly and Clint—tending to Rickles' wound.

WORLD'S BEST PUNCH LINE

～～～

Joe Bologna is a wonderful actor. I've known him for years. He was witness to one of the best moments in my career as a comic. The only problem is that it didn't happen on stage, and it wasn't my line.

It happened when Joe and I were walking in Manhattan and got approached by a homeless guy.

"Got any spare change?" he asked me.

I gave him five bucks.

"Go buy yourself a ranch," I said.

He thanked me, started walking away and then turned back.

"Hey, mister," he said, "now I need cattle."

"Rickles, don't you have a line for this guy?" asked Bologna.

Rickles had nothing, except a great story to tell for the rest of his life.

FAMOUS LAST WORDS

~~~~~~~~

"You're the perfect star for a sitcom, Don," says a famous producer who will remain nameless.

I like flattery as much as the next guy, so I say, "Tell me more."

"You're a natural, Rickles. People like having you in their homes. Why else would Carson and the other talk show hosts have you on so much? You're the average Joe with a wild sense of humor. You love your wife and your kids—that always comes across. And that's the kind of sitcom you should do—head of the household, slightly zany, always getting in jams, but basically a good guy. Isn't that you?"

"I suppose so," I say, "except for one problem."

"What's that?"

"My kind of humor is hard to put in a script. My voice isn't easy to write for. I make it up as I go along. I never know what I'm going to say next. I'm best when I go out there cold. You can't do that in a sitcom."

"Hollywood is full of great writers. You'll find the right one."

Couple of months later, I catch sitcom fever. Producers are interested. ABC is interested. Writers are interested. Scripts are coming in.

Here's the setup: I'm an ad man. My wife's name is Barbara. We have a little girl and a house in the suburbs. I work in the city, and I have a hard time adjusting to the modern world. Funny things happen to me. I'm a funny guy. You gotta like me. You gotta love me. The show has to work, but it doesn't.

"What's wrong?" asks the real-life Barbara when I get home from a hard day at the studio.

"The writing," I say. "It doesn't sound like me."

"Well, tell them."

"I do."

"And what do they say?" asks Barbara.

"They say I'm funny and the writing's funny and the show's a guaranteed hit. The network is convinced."

"And you aren't?"

"I'm convinced I need other writers."

So I get another writer. And then another. And then another after that.

I keep saying, "The story's all right, but where are the laughs?"

"The laughs are there, Don," they say. "They're in the script. They're in the delivery."

Long story short: In 1972, *The Don Rickles Show* hits the airwaves.

Long story even shorter: In 1972, *The Don Rickles Show* is canceled.

Two years later, a certified public accountant starts up his own sitcom.

Ever hear of *The Bob Newhart Show*?

IF AT FIRST YOU DON'T SUCCEED . . .

~~~~~~

"You're a natural star for a sitcom," said a Hollywood producer not long after the *The Don Rickles Show* left the air.

"Where have I heard that before?" I asked.

"A domestic comedy isn't right for you. You're wackier than that, Don. Your humor needs a different backdrop."

"Like what?"

"Like the Navy."

"Why the Navy?"

"You'll make it funny."

"I still worry that it's hard to write for me."

"Remember *Sergeant Bilko?*"

"Sure."

"A genius show, wouldn't you agree?"

"Loved it. I love Phil Silvers."

"Well, what Bilko did for Silvers, this idea will do for you."

Over the next few weeks, the idea took form: As Bilko was a sergeant in the Army, Sharkey was a chief petty officer in the Navy. Bilko had a band of guys under his command. So would Sharkey. They called Silvers' show *Sergeant Bilko*. They were calling mine *C.P.O. Sharkey*.

NBC bought it.

I still worried that it was hard—if not impossible—to write for me, but writers were eager to prove me wrong.

"As Bilko defined TV for the fifties," said one of the trade papers, "Sharkey will define the seventies."

From his typewriter to God's ear.

Turned out that God doesn't read the trades.

It also turned out that Sharkey wasn't a disaster. I liked the guy. He was a crazy Navy chief tailored after my own craziness. The audience liked him enough to keep him around for a couple of years. But I can hardly call it landmark television.

That distinction was reserved for my good friend from Chicago whose low-key psychologist character, like Lucy or Mary or Archie Bunker, will last forever. *The Bob Newhart Show* was brilliant.

Meanwhile, the most memorable moment for Sharkey came from out of the blue.

I had just guest-hosted the *Tonight* show, and, while conducting an interview, I accidentally broke Johnny's favorite cigarette box. Next day on the air, Ed tells Johnny what happened. Johnny decides to have some fun. He has the cameras follow him as he marches out of his studio, down the hallway and bursts onto the soundstage where we're shooting Sharkey. I'm in full Navy dress. Johnny doesn't care.

That's right, I'm C.P.O. Sharkey.

"Rickles," he says, "you busted my cigarette case and you're paying for it."

Johnny goes on and on, raking me over the coals. It's one of Carson's funniest moments, totally spontaneous. I can't stop laughing. I have no quick comeback. Johnny out-Rickles Rickles.

"Ladies and gentlemen," I say when he's through, "Mr. Johnny Carson!"

Johnny shouts back, "They know who I am! You don't have to introduce me."

It's Sharkey's greatest moment: upstaged by King Carson.

KING ELVIS

~~~~~~~

Elvis was huge in the fifties. He had his troubles in the sixties, but he came roaring back in the seventies, when he was huge all over again.

Elvis took over Vegas and made the town his own. When he was playing the Hilton, everyone was happy because business trickled down from his show to everywhere else.

I'd only met the King in passing, but people kept saying he was a big fan of mine. I was flattered but never really believed it. I didn't see Elvis going for my humor.

Then one night, when I'm on stage at the Sahara, there he is. He's with his girlfriend, Linda Thompson, and he's heading for the stage. The audience goes nuts, and all I can say is, "Elvis, it's great to see you. Looks like you got enough gold around your neck to sink the *Titanic.*"

He laughs, but then again he might laugh at anything. His eyes tell me he's feeling no pain.

"Mr. Rickles," he says, "I came up here to help you."

"Thank you, Elvis, I really appreciate it."

"Mr. Rickles, I'm here to bless you. I have a poem I'd like to read in your honor."

"Please do, Elvis."

The poem is flowery and strange and no one knows what it's about. When he's through, I say: "Elvis, we love you. You're a genius and a gentleman for gracing my stage. Now do me a favor. Take your chain, your belt and your cape and go home."

TO THE MOON, ALICE (WITHOUT JACKIE GLEASON)

The seventies were also all about space exploration, a subject that interested me.

It became even more interesting when Barbara and I met Gene Cernan, commander of *Apollo 17*, the fifth and last manned mission to land on the moon. We became friendly, and Gene was nice enough to invite us to the launch—the first night launch in the history of the program. Along with a host of dignitaries and the crew's families, Barb and I had ringside seats at the Kennedy Space Center at Cape Canaveral. A priest gave the prelaunch blessing. I was going to ask why there wasn't a rabbi, but I didn't want to push it.

I had given Gene a tape and asked him to play it for the crew when they landed up there.

"Sure, Don," said Gene. "What's on it?"

"Just a little message for you and the boys," I said.

The mission went well, and months later, after Gene returned safely to earth, we invited him to our home in Beverly Hills.

"Great job, Gene," I said. "America's proud of you. But I'm curious to know how the tape played on the moon. How did the crew react?"

"When we landed, I told the guys, 'Here's an inspiring message from my dear friend Don Rickles.' I turned on the machine and out came a voice that boomed all over the moon: 'Hey, guys, is this trip really necessary? You could have gone to Vegas for a lot less money and left those funny suits at home.' "

Gene was laughing, and I was proud that my voice had made it to the moon.

"For playing that tape, Gene," I said, "I'm treating you to dinner among Hollywood's finest at Chasen's restaurant."

We walked out to the garage. At the time I had a Rolls.

"You're the space commander, Gene," I said. "Why don't you drive?"

"I'd love to," said Gene.

We piled in, Gene turned the key in the ignition and . . . rrrrrrrr . . . . rrrrrrrr . . . .

Nothing.

The Rolls' engine had passed away.

"Lucky we're with the commander," I told Barbara as Gene got out to lift up the hood. He fooled with some wires.

"Try the engine now, Don," said Gene.

I tried.

rrrrrrr . . . . rrrrrrrr . . . .

Still dead.

Still confident, I watched Gene toy with some more wires.

"I think I got it," he said. "It should turn over now."

It didn't. Even the rrrrrrrr was gone.

Gene shut the hood.

"What's the solution, Commander?" I asked.

"Your other car," he said with a smile.

"Wait a minute," I said to my friend. "You can get to the moon in that Buck Rogers space ship, but you can't get to Chasen's in a Rolls-Royce?"

"That seems to be the size of it, Don."

"Why don't you make a long-distance call," I suggest, "so I can hear you say 'Houston, we have a problem.' "

End result: We went to Chasen's in Barbara's Chevy.

Thanks, Bill Harrah, for the good times at Tahoe.

"IF I CAN MAKE THEM LAUGH ON THE MOON, WHY CAN'T I MAKE THEM LAUGH AT HARRAH'S?"

~~~~~

That's what I kept asking my booking agent when he told me that I couldn't work at Bill Harrah's Lake Tahoe resort.

"Bill's a very reserved guy," I was told. "He likes Eddie Arnold, Red Skelton and Jack Benny. People he respects."

"You mean he doesn't respect me?" I asked.

"To be honest," said the agent, "no. You're loud."

"I'll tone it down."

"No you won't. You're incapable of toning it down. Look, Don, forget Harrah's. You're just not Bill Harrah's type of act."

I didn't forget Harrah's, though. I was successful in Vegas and saw no reason why I couldn't be successful in Lake Tahoe.

The agent kept pushing, and finally Bill Harrah relented.

"I'll try him for a week," he said, "and then we'll see."

"Take it easy opening night," the agent advised. "Bill's going to be there. Treat him gently."

Winter in Lake Tahoe.

Opening night.

Rickles on stage.

Bill Harrah in his private booth in the back of the room.

"Mr. Harrah," I said, "I'm not too crazy about your hotel, but I'll do you a favor and work here."

No one ever talked that way to Bill Harrah.

"In fact, this whole resort is ridiculous," I went on. "Why would anyone come up here and pay this kind of money to freeze their burgers off? Besides, Jews don't ski. We own the mountain."

It took Bill a while to react. Meanwhile, management turned green. I got the feeling I had worn out my welcome in the first minute.

But then Bill laughed.

Suddenly everyone was laughing.

From that moment on, I became a Harrah favorite. I played the resort five straight years.

Bill liked to take us out on his boat and sail around Lake Tahoe. Once, when I was with Barbara, Mindy and Larry, he showed us a gorgeous old mansion, right on the lake, where they had filmed the party scene in *The Godfather II*.

"Mindy," I said to my young daughter, "when you grow up, this is where you'll get married." Then I turned to Barbara and said, "That'll make the Corleones very happy."

For my fiftieth birthday, Bill had a little surprise for me.

He drove to our villa in a brand-new silver metallic Corvette Sting Ray.

"Happy Birthday, Don," Bill said. "It's all yours."

"Thanks, Bill," I said, before offering him a few bucks for a cab back to the hotel.

HE READS THE *NEW YORK TIMES*

~~~~~~

I read the *New York Post*.

He studies the editorials.

I study the sports page.

He likes polite discourse.

I'm loud.

So how the hell have we come to like each other so much?

We make each other laugh—that's how.

Offstage, I'm Bob Newhart's best audience and he's mine. It helps, of course, that our wives have maintained their close friendship. Bob and I both subscribe to the philosophy that has saved many a marriage: Happy wife, happy life.

For some thirty-five years, the Newharts and the Rickleses have taken many happy vacations together. We've traveled the world. I've watched him hide as I've made fun of people in foreign languages I don't understand. He's watched me doze off while he's discussed the world's problems. My problem was finding out if the Dodgers beat the Giants.

We once went to Spain and stayed in a private villa that had two sleeping quarters. One was a suite. The other wasn't. Ginnie, who's wonderful, said, "Bob, let's give the Rickleses the suite."

Bob wanted to flip for it. Ginnie said, "No, they're our friends and they get the suite."

The suite was fabulous. The Newharts' room wasn't. To get to their bathroom, they had to walk through our suite.

"You're bothering us, Bob," I'd tell him when he hurried through. "You're ruining our vacation."

Once, in the Hong Kong airport, we waited for our luggage. It was a madhouse, a sea of people, all scrambling to find their suitcases and trunks.

The usual procedure was this: Bob and Barbara would identify the luggage and deal with the customs officials while Ginnie and I found a comfortable bench and watched.

So the mess in Hong Kong hadn't put Bob in a great mood.

"Hey, Bob," I said, "while you're sorting out luggage, see if any of those Chinese guys want to do our laundry."

We often attracted American tourists.

Once in Germany, walking through some village, we were approached by a church group from Iowa.

"Look, Don," said Bob. "Let's be nice, but let's not get into a long conversation. I don't want to spend my afternoon talking about our TV shows."

"Me either," I said.

The first tourist who comes up starts gushing about *The Bob Newhart Show*. I expect Bob to politely blow him off. But when the guy asks a specific question about one of the episodes, Bob gets into a long conversation.

"Hey," I say afterward, "I thought we weren't going to talk to the tourists."

"They would have asked about your shows," Bob says, "but no one remembers them."

We're in Venice, where Bob and I have a ringside table on the Piazza San Marco. We're not wine drinkers, but to blend in with the scenery we order a bottle that we have no plans to touch. Our big plan is to people-watch. As the crowd passes by, we invent stories: There's Count Borinsky from Russia; there's Princess Magala from Spain; there's Prince Eric of Norway with Sylvia Borstein from the Bronx on his arm. They're having a torrid affair.

All the while, people are feeding the pigeons. In fact, the pigeons are so well fed that when we leave the birds circle us and drop farewell messages on our shoulders, making us look like Italian generals.

The Newharts invite us over every Christmas eve. They have the big tree, the wreaths, the angels and the carols.

Once in a while, Bob has a serious moment and says to me, "Don, you really enjoy Christmas, don't you?"

"Sure I do. One of our guys started it."

"Bob, believe me, you're funny."

POACHED EGGS

～～～

I've always respected the comedians who came before me. Milton Berle's delivery was dynamite. No one was more lovable than George Burns—and no one more popular than Bob Hope.

Hope had me on his shows many times. Unlike me, Bob didn't like to improvise. As a matter of fact, he relied on a small army of writers. Everything with Hope had to be rehearsed a lot. He worked with big cardboard cue signs.

At the start of one routine we were rehearsing, my line was, "Hi, Bob."

Bob stopped the rehearsal.

"Is that how you're going to say the line when we tape?" he asked.

"Yes," I answered.

"Try it again."

"Hi, Bob," I said.

"We better meet with the writers," Hope said.

We went into Bob's office, where three writers sat on a couch.

"Okay," said Hope, "say it for them, Don."

"Hi, Bob," I repeated.

"I don't like the inflection," Bob said. "What else can we do with the line?"

The writers proceeded to give me six alternative inflections on "Hi, Bob." I thought it was all a joke, but no one was laughing.

My biggest Hope moment didn't come on his show. It happened on Dean Martin's show when I was standing in front of dozens of stars. The idea was that I'd rib each of them for three minutes. At the end of the routine, Hope, who was famous for entertaining our troops the world over, slipped into a back seat.

"Bob Hope is here," I said. "I guess the war is over."

Of that older generation, I adored Jack Benny. To this day, I love imitating him in front of my friends. When it came to timing, Jack was the master. He used silence the way Picasso used paint. His patented gesture—putting his hand under his chin and slowly turning his head—was the most beautiful movement in all comedy.

I was excited when he came to my show for the first time. It happened at the Sahara. By then, he was getting up in years, but he hadn't lost any of his charm. He'd never come to my shows, because he didn't think my humor was his cup of tea. But George Burns, Jack's dearest friend and a supporter of mine, finally persuaded Jack to see me in person.

After the show at the Sahara, Jack came to my dressing room and said, "Don"—I loved that inflection of his when he

"Relax, Jack. I'll get you a light."
Looking on are my pals Ed McMahon and Joey Bishop.

said "Don"—"I enjoyed your show. You really surprised me."

"Gee, Jack," I said, "coming from you, that's about the nicest compliment of my life. Will you join me and Barbara for dinner?"

"I'd love to."

We took him to the House of Lords, the hotel's finest restaurant.

"Jack," I said, "it's a real pleasure. Order whatever you like."

I ordered a vodka martini.

Barbara ordered a vodka martini with a lemon twist.

Jack asked for a glass of water.

"That's it?" I asked him.

"That's it."

For dinner, I ordered the veal Milanese.

Barbara ordered the filet mignon.

With his stop-and-start deadpan delivery, Jack said, "I'll have . . . two poached eggs." Big pause. "And one slice of toast."

"That's it?" I asked.

"That's it," Jack answered.

Dessert: chocolate soufflé for me; tiramisu for Barbara.

For Jack?

Hot tea. With lemon.

"Look, Don," he said, "you and Barbara have been most gracious, and this place is delightful. I don't want to disappoint you, but nothing makes me happier than two poached eggs." Big pause. "And a slice of toast."

At that moment—don't ask me why—I loved Jack Benny even more.

A KID FROM THE NEIGHBORHOOD

~~~~~~

That's who I am.

That's who I'll always be.

So when a kid from the neighborhood learns he's going to the White House, he's excited.

Doesn't matter who the President is—the President could be a peanut farmer—but the kid's still excited.

In fact, the President *was* a peanut farmer. Jimmy Carter was the man, and me, Barbara and our kids were off to Washington to meet him. Bob Newhart had arranged it, and it was going to be a family affair. He was bringing Ginnie and their kids. We were all thrilled.

"Be low-key," Bob kept telling me. "This is the White House."

"Hey, Bob, I know the difference between the White House and the White Castle, where they give you a bag of burgers for a buck."

When we arrived, we were greeted by Zbigniew Brzezinski, national security adviser to the President.

"The President is looking forward to meeting you all," said Mr. Brzezinski.

As we walked down toward the Oval Office, several officials stopped us.

"The President is waiting to meet you," they said.

We bumped into Vice President Walter Mondale. "I understand you're going to meet the President," he said.

When we got to the Oval Office, Carter's secretary was there to meet us.

"I'm afraid the President just stepped out," she said. "He should be right back. Would you like to take a look in his office?"

Sure.

We stepped inside. It looked just the way it looks in the movies. Not a scrap of paper on his desk. On the back of the big swivel chair behind his desk was a grey cardigan sweater.

"That's his sweater," said the secretary.

Bob looked at me.

I looked at Bob.

The President's sweater wasn't all that thrilling.

"Will the President be back shortly?" we asked.

"He should," said the secretary. "He'd like to say hello to all of you."

We waited for a minute or two, but no President. Outside the Oval Office, we waited a little while longer. No President.

"Where is he, ma'am?" I asked.

"He heard you were coming," said Bob, "and he must have gotten nervous and left."

Back in Los Angeles, everyone asked me, "Did you meet the President?"

"No," I said, "but I made friends with his sweater."

"Bob and Bruce, how do I know if your albums will sell?"

ROCK AND ROLL RICKLES

~~~~~~~

As time went on, President Carter wasn't the only celebrity dying to meet me. The biggest rock-and-roll star since Elvis had busted out, and my son, Larry, was dying to see him. I pulled some strings and we were off to see Bruce Springsteen.

Since I'm a Vegas kind of guy, I didn't have any background in big-time rock shows. I didn't know what to expect. I didn't know we needed fourteen badges and eighteen wristbands to get past the thirty-two security guards to get to our seats in the VIP area. I didn't know that the twenty loudspeakers onstage would be blasting out more noise than atomic bombs. I didn't know that the show would go on for three hours, getting louder by the minute.

Didn't know that his fans sitting around us would be screaming even before the show started.

Didn't know that to meet Bruce we'd have to wait outside his dressing room for two hours without food or water.

When we were finally escorted in, I saw this extremely kind and sweet man wearing a bandana around his forehead. He looked like a pirate.

"Great show, Bruce," I said.

"Hope you'll come to another one," he said.

"What?" I said. "I can't hear you."

I'd gone deaf.

MOBY DICK

~~~~~~~

In spite of the volume, I really liked the Springsteen show. I could see why his fans were so loyal. But of course loyalty for me always goes back to Sinatra.

In the eighties, we became even closer. When Frank married his Barbara, he finally found a stable domestic life. They loved entertaining and were fabulous hosts. We loved when we were invited to their place in Palm Springs for the weekend. Everyone called it the Compound.

The Compound was spacious and relaxed. The guest quarters were separate from the main house. Guests were given a beautiful bedroom and private bath. There was a fully stocked kitchen and lots of help to make sure you were comfortable.

After you settled in, Frank called you to the main house, where he'd be listening to music in the den. Drinks were served and the fun began.

One Easter weekend, we were there with three other couples: Veronique and Gregory Peck, Luisa and Roger Moore, and Jolene and George Schlatter.

"Rib Peck," Frank urged me. "Try to shake him up a little."

"Captain Ahab," I said to Greg in my best Peck voice, "the sea is stormy, the sailors are restless."

Peck, of course, played Ahab in the movie *Moby Dick*.

Greg went along with it, and Frank thought my kibitzing was hilarious.

"More," Sinatra urged me out of the side of his mouth, "you're getting to him."

"Take it easy, Frank. I don't want to upset the guy."

"Relax, Rickles," said Sinatra, "I got you covered."

"We've sighted the whale, sir!" I shouted to Greg. "To the harpoons!"

Greg half-smiled.

Next day, I was lounging by the pool when Frank came over and sat next to me.

"When Peck gets out here," he said, "this time really lay it on him. It makes him crazy."

"Gee, Frank," I replied, "I like the man."

"Hey, I know Greg," said Sinatra. "He secretly loves it."

So like a dummy, to make Frank happy, I continued.

"Captain Ahab!" I shouted as soon as Gregory appeared, his little dog running behind him. "The men are in mutiny. There's trouble on deck."

As I got up to give Peck a captain's salute, his little dog ran under my chair. When I sat down, the dog's tail got entangled in the chair and he yelped like crazy. I jumped up to free the dog.

"Look at this," Frank said to Greg, "now the man's attacking your dog."

Greg looked at Frank, then looked at me, then picked up his dog and hurried off.

A few days later, Greg sent flowers to me and Barbara and a kind letter of apology for leaving abruptly. But Frank kept saying, "See what you did to Captain Ahab, Don? If his dog dies, you're in real trouble."

During the Saturday night dinner Frank said, "I think it'd be nice if we all went to church tomorrow."

"Frank," I said, "I'd really prefer to sit by the pool. You may have heard, I'm Jewish."

"Don't worry, the priest is a personal friend."

That night, Sinatra was in an especially good mood and the pre-Easter celebration went on till the wee small hours.

Next morning, we woke up, got dressed and the four of us—me, Barbara and the Moores—walked to the main house to meet Mr. and Mrs. S.

But Mr. S. never showed.

"He's decided to sleep in," said his Barbara, "but he wants us all to go."

We went to the church. We sat in the first pew. We listened to the music. We listened to the sermon. I can't say I was all that comfortable, but respect is respect.

When it came time to put money in the basket, I dropped in fifty dollars and Roger nodded approvingly.

"You gave for everyone," said Roger. "Happy Easter, Don."

How about that? It costs me fifty bucks to be Catholic. And Frank was still in bed singing "My Way."

"CAN THE PRINCE COME OUT AND PLAY?"

~~~~~~

The Sinatras and the Rickleses also spent time together on the Riviera in Monte Carlo. Frank's great pal and restaurateur, Jilly Rizzo, was there as well.

"Look, Don," Jilly told me, "you see how your suite overlooks Frank's? Well, every morning I'll come out on his balcony and signal you. If you see me waving a pink handkerchief, that means Frank's sleeping. Stay where you are. But if I'm waving a white handkerchief, come down and we'll go to the beach."

We didn't know whether we were on vacation or hiding out from the police.

Frank had a private cabana, a big tent covered on every side. I couldn't see out.

"Hey, Frank," I said, "I have fans and they can't see me."

"We need our privacy," said Frank.

"You need your privacy. You're Frank Sinatra. I need someone to wave at me. I need to be recognized."

"Eat, Bullethead, and cut out the jokes."

All day, the food kept coming—salami, cheeses, pasta. Enough food to put you in the hospital.

We dined with our wives. As the hour got late, though, the wives decided to retire while Frank urged the boys on.

He had his driver take us to the palace where Prince Albert of Monaco lived. Frank had me and Jilly get out of the car and start shouting, "Can the prince come out and play?"

The guards tried to keep a straight face. But once they saw it was Sinatra, they would get Albert. Albert, always accompanied by a security guard, loved to hang out with Frank. Who didn't?

We hit all the jet-set spots.

Next thing you know, it's three in the morning and we find ourselves sitting in the corner of an empty club listening to a piano player sing "As Time Goes By." I think I'm in the "Play it again, Sam" scene of *Casablanca*.

"The sound's wrong," says Sinatra. "The guy's singing great, but his loudspeakers are too close together."

Frank has me and Jilly standing on ladders rehanging the speakers.

"Two inches to the left," he tells me. "An inch to the right," he tells Jilly.

He's finally pleased with the sound but ready to move on. Next stop is the Hotel de Paris. We're sitting at a beautiful bar facing a huge bay window. Suddenly a storm comes up; lightning is flashing across the sky.

"Get out there," says Frank, "and tell the paparazzi to stop taking my picture."

"It's pouring rain, Frank," we say. "It's lightning."

"Get out there and tell them!"

Jilly and I run out in the rain and tell the lightning to stop taking Frank's picture.

Next morning, the white hankie is waving and we're invited to breakfast. Frank's at the beach. He's in his white trousers, white shirt, blue blazer and captain's hat tilted to the side. Standing on a rock, he looks like he stepped out of a page from *Gentlemen's Quarterly*. Suddenly a wave hits the rock and splashes on Frank's beautiful outfit. Sinatra gets crazy and blames us.

That night he invites us to dinner at the restaurant on the balcony of the Hotel de Paris. We're all decked out.

But at the next table, a guy's wearing a short-sleeve shirt and no jacket.

Frank whispers to Jilly, "This guy's not properly dressed. Ask him to leave."

Jilly goes over and somehow convinces the guy to change tables, out of Frank's sight.

"It's taken care of," says Jilly when he returns.

"Great," says Frank, " 'cause I was about to smack him."

Believe me, Sinatra wasn't about to do it, but he felt good when he said it.

Our last day on the Riviera with Frank and Barbara.

"Special treat," says Sinatra, "we're taking you to a garden party at the palace."

My Barbara and I are delighted. The palace grounds, high on a hill overlooking the Monaco Harbor, are magnificent. The sun's shining and the crowd is wall-to-wall royalty.

Of course, I don't know who's who. This one's a count; that one's a countess; this one's father owns Portugal; that one's uncle fell into a bucket of oil money.

During high tea, we're served a lovely assortment of pastries.

I'm on my best behavior.

Seated next to me is a distinguished-looking woman. I figure her for a duchess.

"I'm Don Rickles," I say. "Nice to meet you, madam."

"My pleasure, Mr. Rickles. My name is Estée Lauder."

"Wow," I say, "I thought you were a sign."

My Barbara gives me a look, but Estée Lauder gives me a laugh.

Our Riviera trip has a fairy-tale ending: We all live happily ever after.

THE LADIES WHO LIVE IN CONDOS

Frank was good enough to introduce me to Prince Albert.

Bob Hope introduced me to Princess Margaret.

It happened in London. Hope emceed a show to entertain the Princess at the Grosvenor House. The Newharts were there. So were Telly Savalas, Sean Connery and Jack Hawkins. It was a gala event.

Newhart kept warning me. "The English have a different sense of humor," he said. "So I suggest you take it easy."

Hope was even more nervous. When he introduced me, he apologized like crazy, saying, "Ladies and gentlemen, Don Rickles is a different kind of comic. He might say something that sounds insulting, but he doesn't mean it. Don't take it personally."

"I understand the Queen Mum takes in laundry," I said when I get on stage. "She realizes your country owes us a lot of money. I understand that Queen Elizabeth and her husband what's-his-name are renting out two rooms in the palace. It's a damn shame it's come to this."

After the show, I was sitting with Hope when the Princess's special guard with white gloves approached our table.

"The Princess would like to see you," he said.

I stood up and Hope prepared to go with me.

"Just Mr. Rickles," said the guard.

As I was escorted to the private booth, I wondered whether my act had gone over with her.

"Your majesty," I said.

"Please, call me ma'am. You were very entertaining, Mr. Rickles, but you were so quick that certain remarks got by me."

"Thank you, ma'am. Next time I'll slow down."

"I'd appreciate that," she said. "What would you like to drink?"

"Vodka, please."

"Excellent. I'm having a double gin."

I smiled inwardly. This was my kind of lady.

The drinks came.

"May I offer a toast to England, ma'am?" I asked.

"To England indeed."

The Princess got a little chatty.

"I understand that your mother is eighty-three years old," she said.

"She is."

"Well, my mum is also eighty-three."

"That's a nice coincidence, ma'am." My God, I think to myself, she's talking about the Queen Mother!

"I also understand that your mother suffers from emphysema."

"Unfortunately," I said.

"Unfortunately my mother also suffers from emphysema."

"I'm sorry to hear that, ma'am."

"They tell me your mother has a beautiful place in Florida."

"Yes, she does."

"God bless your mother," said the Princess. "And God bless mine. She also has a beautiful place right down the street."

"The only difference, ma'am, is that your mother's place has a flag on the roof."

"Roy, don't ever say Dean can't sing."

"IT'S THAT SLOW IN VEGAS?"

My mother was my heart.

She believed in me from day one. On those days when the world said no, Mom said yes.

Her steady message was, "You'll get there, Don darling, I know you will."

She knew what I didn't. She had certainty when I had doubts.

And talk about strong! Don't even think about getting in her way.

I remember when Barbara and I first got married, we lived in our own apartment right next to Mom's. Sometimes a few days would go by and I wouldn't see my mother. Then I'd come home to find a note under my door:

"What's the matter," the note read, "we're not talking any more?" Signed, "Mom."

Etta Rickles would have loved to be a performer. Her Sophie Tucker imitation was priceless and, believe me, better than mine.

Etta Rickles, seventy-four years young.

When I was featured on Ralph Edwards' *This Is Your Life* TV show, Mom was living in Miami Beach and couldn't make it to California. So they had a remote camera on her.

"Don, dear," she told me in front of the national audience, "I have chopped liver waiting on the table for you, Ralph Edwards and all your friends."

When Barbara, the kids and I stayed at the Eden Roc, not far from Mom's condo, we knew that we couldn't miss early-bird dinner with her, every day, promptly at five. Even as she got older, Etta ruled the roost.

She dyed her hair red. She thought it looked great. I thought it was too red, but I never said anything. I told Barbara, though, "If Mom were seventy-five years younger, she'd look like Orphan Annie."

In her eighties, my mother's body began to fail. We visited her often, and her spirit was always positive. If anyone could beat any disease, it was my mother.

Then one night I was performing in Nevada when the call came.

"She's very ill," said her doctor. "You better come."

I arrived at the hospital in Miami Beach, where she had the nurses running in every direction. They adored her, though. Everyone did.

When I entered her room, I was shocked to see a half-dozen tubes attached to her. She looked pale and tired, but she managed a smile when she saw me.

I leaned over and said, "Mom, dear, I'm here."

"Don, darling. Is it that slow in Vegas?" She took my hand and she gave it a little squeeze. "Tell me," she said. "Tell me something good."

I told her that my career was doing well, that Barbara and the children were healthy and more beautiful than ever, that we were all blessed to have her in our life.

"Don't forget me," she said.

"I think of you every day. And I always will."

And I always have.

On September 22, 1984, Etta Rickles went home to God.

"What? We're not honoring Jack Benny?"

BUCKET OF BELUGA

~~~~~~

January 1985.

I was with Barbara and the kids in Hawaii when I got paged by the pool.

Sinatra was on the line. "I need you in D.C. day after tomorrow, Bullethead. Bring Barbara. This is the big show."

"What show, Frank?"

"Reagan's second inauguration. I'm giving you a featured spot."

Frank was wonderful that way. He did all kinds of good things for people without the press knowing. He'd do anything for his friends.

Reagan and I had been friends since he was governor. He always got a kick out of me ribbing him on one of those Dean Martin TV roasts.

I was ready. We packed up and flew to Washington, only to learn that Sinatra had to insist that Rickles be on the show.

"Who knows what Rickles is gonna say?" asked one official.

"Anything he says will be funny," said Frank.

"I'm not sure," said the official.

"I am," said Frank. "That's that."

Thanks to Frank, I was in.

I wound up in a small dressing room on the ground floor of the convention center where the show was being broadcast on national TV. When Frank found out, he told security, "Get Bullethead up here with me and Dean right now."

I walked into the fancy dressing room where Dean and Frank gave me big hugs.

"No drinking before the show," said Frank as he stepped out for a minute.

"No worries, pally," said Dean, opening his tux jacket to reveal a supply of little airline bottles.

I downed one of them and headed for the stage.

This was not your usual audience. The President and Nancy were sitting only a few feet away.

I thought I'd be introduced by Frank, or Tom Selleck, or Jimmy Stewart. Instead I was introduced by Emmanuel Lewis, the small African-American kid who played Webster on TV.

With a deadpan face, the kid turned to me and said, "Be funny."

"Great," I said, "I'm brought out here by the first black man who will never play basketball in the NBA."

Then I did Rickles:

"I just saw Vice President George Bush out in the lobby, going 'No one recognizes me. No one knows me.'

"I must tell you, Mr. President," I added, "it's a big treat coming out here all the way from California for this kind of money."

With that, I dropped the microphone on the floor.

When I picked it up, I saw Secretary of State George Shultz sitting in the first row. "Great to see you, sir, but why are you here? Do something. Go over to the Russian embassy and have a bucket of Beluga."

I spotted Charlton Heston. "If he's Moses," I told the audience, "I'm a Mau Mau fighter pilot. Heston, it's over."

Then I turned to the President and said, "Is this too fast for you, Ronnie? Please, Mr. President, try not to nap when I'm talking. Why don't you and Nancy go out to the lobby and practice the waltz. I'll call you when the show's over. But really, folks, it's an honor to be here. Personally, I voted for Herbert Hoover, but I'm still happy to entertain a President who was the best host General Electric ever had."

BARBARA BUSH AND
BIKINI BEACH

~~~~

Once, I saw President Reagan in swim trunks on the beach near our house in Malibu. He was surrounded by a dozen guys in black suits talking into their wrists. I went right up to him. He motioned the security men to let me by.

"Good morning, Don," he said.

"Good morning, Mr. President."

"Beautiful morning, isn't it?" he asked, motioning to the clear blue sky and pounding waves.

"Gorgeous," I answered.

"Makes me think back to when I was a lifeguard. Did you know I was a great swimmer, Don?"

"Really?"

"I had a great backstroke and a fantastic crawl."

Can you imagine? The President of the United States was talking like I was his swimming instructor. All I needed was a whistle and someone to save.

• • •

Another time Barbara and I were eating at Chasen's in Beverly Hills with a group of friends when Nancy and the President came in. They walked over to our table.

"Don, great to see you," said the President.

"Great to see you, too, Mr. President."

My friends were really impressed. "My God, Don," said one, "the President really made a fuss over you. You must be excited."

"No big deal," I said as I started to eat and put my fork in my eye.

Reagan wasn't the only President who liked me. I'm proud to say that George Bush the First was also a fan.

He invited us to the White House for a state dinner. He never even told me to watch my behavior.

Lovely affair. I sat next to Barbara Bush. The President was one table over. Mrs. Bush is a spirited woman. She insisted that I call her Barbara.

"Don," she said, "I've followed your career."

"Gee, Barbara, I'm flattered."

"I know you were in that submarine movie with Burt Lancaster and Clark Gable. I know you did some *Twilight Zone*s and some fine television dramas. But there's one question I've always wanted to ask you, Don."

"By all means, Barbara."

"Were things so bad that you had to do *Bikini Beach* and *Beach Blanket Bingo?*"

Mrs. Bush is something else.

EVERYONE WANTS TO MEET THE POPE

~~~~~~

I don't care if your name is Hymie Shlosstein, you want to meet the Pope. What else are you going to do in Italy besides eat ravioli and stare at women?

It's fun meeting movie stars, fun meeting famous athletes, a kick meeting powerful politicians, but the Pope . . . well, the Pope is Pope.

I wanted to meet the Pope.

My dear friend Carroll O'Connor said he'd arrange it.

"Thanks, pal," I said as Barbara and I packed our bags and met the Newharts at the airport.

"Carroll set it up," I told Bob. "We're in."

A few days later, we're escorted through the Vatican. Naturally we're excited. The guards open a door and I expect to see the Pope at his desk. I see the Pope, but he's about two football fields away. I need binoculars to make sure it's him. Between him and us are two thousand people. We're asked to take a seat.

"Hey, Archie, who told you I was Jewish?"

They're chanting in Latin, Spanish, Polish and French. The chanting is pretty except I have to go to the bathroom. When I get up, though, a guard says I can't leave while the people are chanting and the Pope is praying.

"Well, I'm praying that he stops praying soon," I tell the guard. "Maybe you haven't noticed, but I'm turning blue."

"How was your visit to the Vatican?" asks Carrroll when I get home to California.

"Beautiful," I say. "I was as close to him as I am to you."

"But I'm calling from New York," says O'Connor.

"That's the idea."

I didn't drop the idea of meeting the Pope. Next trip to Italy, Barbara and I had a guide. Let's call him Guido. Guido takes us everywhere. He knows everything, all the history, all the people.

"Guido," I say, "you're terrific. Is it possible to meet the Pope?"

"Sure, but it'll cost you."

Figures. I hand over the money and the next thing I know we're back in the Vatican.

We walk up to the private entrance where the famous guards with the spears are standing.

"This way," says Guido. We walk up some stairs leading to the Pope's private quarters. The door opens and there's a man in a red robe and a skull cap manufactured by my people.

"He's a monsignor," Guido explains.

"I'm honored," I say. "Is the Pope in residence?"

"I'm afraid not," says the monsignor.

"May I ask where is he?"

"He's at his summer home."

The monsignor is a kind man. He takes us on a tour of the papal quarters. The kitchen is done in four shades of linoleum. But who's going to question the Pope's taste?

We go to a room that leads out to the balcony where the Pope blesses the people.

"I can do that," I say. "If Reagan can play President, I can play Pope."

I start heading out on the balcony when the monsignor says, "Please, Mr. Rickles, only the Holy Father walks through those doors."

"Sorry, I just wanted to feed the pigeons."

He takes me to the Pope's bedroom and gives me one of his tall hats.

"Thank you so much," I say, "I'll cherish this forever, but I'm looking at those crosses in his jewelry box and wondering if he has an extra one for my friend Frank Sinatra."

The monsignor opens a drawer filled with crosses and hands me one. "This one has been kissed and blessed by the Pope," he promises.

"Frank will love it."

Frank does love it.

"He actually handed it to you?" Frank asks when I give him the cross next time I see him.

"One of his guys handed it to me," I say.

"So you didn't get to meet the Pope?"

"No, but I got an eight-by-ten glossy of him, saying 'Love ya,' Frank. Signed 'Pope.' "

END OF AN ERA

~~~~~~

My manager Joe Scandore was one of a kind. He came out of that era when a man's word was his bond and loyalty was everything. He took me on when I needed a boost. Back when no one but Mom thought I'd ever make it, Joe said, "Don, I'm betting on you."

Joe had a great presence. He owned the Elegante in Brooklyn. He booked acts. He discovered talent. He cut deals. He was old-school show biz. Like any savvy promoter who came up in the thirties and forties, Joe had connections outside formal show business. That was the way of the world. Without those connections, you never left the dock; with them, you sailed.

When he died in the late eighties, his friends came out to honor him. At his funeral, the Brooklyn cathedral was packed to the rafters. As I sat in my front-row pew, I heard people say, "Hey, there's Louie Zambatone. When did he get out?"

Some of his friends showed up late and couldn't get in. These were people who didn't like being turned away.

A guy named Mike was at the door, and once the church was filled to capacity, he was told to keep everyone else out.

Some of Joe's friends weren't happy.

The priest, though, went on with the service, chanting and praying and lighting candles.

Meanwhile, from the back of the church I heard someone shout as the door opened, "Let me in there or I'll take your cousin by his macaronis and break your uncle's arms."

"Let us pray," said the priest, "for a man of peace, a good friend and a sweet soul whose legacy of good work will live on."

"I'll run my car over your daughter's face," yelled another gentleman as he was turned away from the door. "Let me in that church or I'll take your mother's eyes out."

"We take time," said the priest, "to give tribute to a man of integrity, faith and goodwill."

"You good-for-nothing sausage," an unhappy guest yelled at Mike, "get off my foot and let me in!"

The verbal jousting went on, but Mike held his ground. Inside, the tributes continued. When services were over and it was time to take Joe to his final resting place, I wondered if those friends who hadn't gotten in would show up at the cemetery. They did. Staying a few discreet feet behind a motorcycle cop, their Cadillacs and Lincolns were part of the procession. When we got to the grave site, I heard one friendly voice tell Mike, "If you try to keep me out of this service, I'll bury you."

I GOT A HORSE RIGHT HERE . . .

~~~~~~

Certain guys I loved. Certain guys I'll always love.

Don Adams was one of those guys.

Don and I went back to the very beginnings at the Wayne Room in Washington. We'd known each other for centuries.

Don was a good guy. I made appearances on his TV show, *Get Smart*, along with Jimmy Caan. The three of us became pals, and Don was always pushing me to go to the track.

I'm no gambler, but the track reminds me of my dad, so I have good associations.

One Saturday afternoon, Don dragged me out to Hollywood Park.

"Got a special surprise for you, Rickles," he said.

"What's that?"

"Look up at the board."

I saw the name, but I had to be seeing wrong. So I rubbed my eyes and looked again. There it was, plain as day: Listed among the other horses was one called Don Rickles.

Don Adams, a friend to remember.

"You gotta put something on him," urged Adams.

"Can he run? Is he good?" I asked.

"What do I know?" asked Adams.

"You know everything about the horses," I said. "I know nothing."

"You know that Don Rickles is the most beautiful name in the world. That name deserves to have good money riding on it."

"Anybody betting on Rickles?" I asked around.

"You kidding?" someone answered. "He's a long shot. My money's on the favorite."

"How 'bout you, Adams?" I asked.

"I never say who I'm betting on before I bet."

"All right," I said, "I'll put a couple of bucks on Don Rickles."

"A couple of bucks!" said Adams. "That's all you think you're worth?"

"Fine," I sighed. "I'll go crazy. A hundred bucks."

Don Rickles ran fourth.

While I tore up my ticket, Adams trotted over to the payout window to cash in his winnings. He had the favorite.

"You look unhappy, Don," said Adams.

"No, I'm thrilled," I said. "This is just what I needed—a day at the races."

"I'll cheer you up," Adams promised. "Come with me."

Don took us to the winner's circle where a garland of flowers was being put around the favorite's neck.

"Can I borrow these flowers for a second?" Adams asked the owner.

Before the owner could answer, Don took the garland and put it on Don Rickles the horse.

"Don Rickles," he said to me, "stand next to Don Rickles."

He snapped a picture.

"Don Rickles," he said, "now you're the winner."

YOU GOTTA LOVE CLINT EASTWOOD

What other movie star would invite you to ridicule him in front of President Clinton?

That's just what Clint did. It was at the Kennedy Center Honors. Morgan Freeman, Forest Whitaker and I sang and danced on stage, giving tribute to the man we had worked with. I could see by the gleam in Clinton's eye that he wanted to grab his sax and join us, but the President restrained himself.

I didn't.

"Mr. President and Mrs. President," I said. "I am here tonight because of you. I couldn't care less about Clint.

"Why do I make fun of you, Clint?" I asked. "Because you have no personality."

I ended by confessing the truth: I love the guy. He can write, act and direct.

Now if he'd only stop giving boxing lessons at the girls' gym . . .

CASINO

~~~~~~~~

Big production.

Big director: Marty Scorsese.

Big writer: Nicholas Pileggi.

Big cast: Robert De Niro, Sharon Stone, Joe Pesci, James Woods, Alan King.

Big deal for me: De Niro runs the casino and I'm his number-one man. I'm with him night and day.

The big deal happens in the nineties when a lot of good things start happening to me. Of course, good things happened in the eighties—and the seventies, sixties and fifties for that matter. The business has always been good to me. But when I approached seventy, I couldn't help wondering whether the jobs would dry up. Thank God, they didn't.

The *Casino* gig was great. I was excited to be working with all these Academy Award winners. No one does gangster films better than Scorsese. And because Vegas had been my territory for many decades, I felt comfortable on the set.

"It isn't so much what you say that makes you right for this part, Don," said Marty. "It's who you are."

I wasn't sure I should take that as a compliment, but I did.

As shooting began, I played it loose. I started kidding from the outset.

"When you direct me, Marty," I said, "could you stand on a chair so I can see you? If it helps, I'll get a telephone book to put under your feet."

First day of shooting had some brief dialogue between me and De Niro. I was standing right next to Bob but acted like I couldn't understand him.

"Could you ask Bob to speak more clearly," I said to Marty.

I heard someone in the crew sarcastically whisper, "Lots of luck."

The scene went on and I tried to get in the mood, but I couldn't stop kibitzing. It's fun to rib De Niro because, fine actor that he is, he takes everything seriously.

"He's mumbling, Marty," I told Scorsese. "The man has won every acting award in America, France and Bulgaria, and he's mumbling. I can't understand him. Can you understand him?" I asked the lighting man who shook his head no. "Can you understand that mumbling?" I asked the cameraman who also said no. "How about you?" I asked the wardrobe girl. "Can you understand him?" She went along with me and shook her head no.

"We got a problem here, Marty," I said. "We got an actor who's ruining your eighty-million-dollar picture. Is there a speech teacher on the set? We have an award-winning actor who's lousing up the movie."

In one scene, Pesci beat me up with a telephone. He got so carried away that when Marty yelled "Cut!" Pesci went looking for a gun.

If you see the movie, I'm in dozens of scenes, but I hardly speak.

"What's wrong?" I asked Marty. "So far I say nothing."

"I see you more as a presence rather than a talker."

"That's a twist," I said. "A silent Rickles. But will the world buy it?"

The world didn't seem to mind. The movie was a hit. I even got good reviews. Around the same time, I got another good role. No, it wasn't Shylock in *The Merchant of Venice* or King Lear.

It was Mr. Potato Head.

An entire career, and I end up with two toys.

PEACEFUL AFTERNOON
IN MALIBU . . .

~~~~~~

The sky's blue, the ocean's calm.

I'm at our beach house, just taking it easy.

John Lasseter, a director of animated movies, is on his way to see me. I figure it's gotta be something big.

When John arrives, he says, "Don, I'm here to test your voice."

"Test my voice, what for?"

He says he's doing *Toy Story*.

"Count me out," I say.

"You haven't heard about the part," John argues.

"I don't do Popeye," I say.

"It's not Popeye."

"I don't do Olive Oyl."

"It's not Olive Oyl."

"I don't do Snoopy."

"You couldn't do Snoopy if you wanted to."

"I don't want to," I say. "I don't want to do Pocahontas' brother."

"Don, listen to me."

"John, leave me alone, will you? I'm trying to keep my name alive here. You want to turn me into Mickey Mouse."

"This movie's going to be huge."

"So is my ego, and my ego says I need to be seen, not just heard."

"Will you let me describe the part?" John asks.

"Go ahead, I'm listening."

"It's Mr. Potato Head."

"Terrific. But I'm not sure I can handle the dramatic demands."

"Mr. Potato Head is a sarcastic wise guy. Think you can handle that?"

That got me thinking.

When the film came out and broke all kinds of box office records, I stopped thinking. I became a hero to a whole generation of children. Even today my own grandchildren aren't impressed that I've played Vegas for fifty years, but they are impressed that their Pop-Pop is Mr. Potato Head.

Soon after the premiere, I called John and asked him, "When's *Toy Story 2* coming up?"

"Soon," he said.

"Great," I said. "Count me in. I've always wanted to do kids' movies."

BLEEDING DODGER BLUE

～～～

As a kid growing up in New York, I loved the Giants. When I moved to L.A, though, I switched loyalties to the Dodgers.

For over forty years now, I've been bleeding Dodger blue.

I've suffered and celebrated with the Dodgers during the Koufax-Drysdale sixties, the Garvey-Cey seventies, the Valenzuela-Hershiser eighties and the Piazza-Karros nineties. I follow every catch, every pitch, every play.

I even became pals with manager Tommy Lasorda.

Lasorda loves Hollywood as much as Hollywood loves him. He was close to Sinatra, another big Dodger fan, and had an open-door policy when it came to celebrities.

After the game, he liked having people in his office. If the Dodgers won that day, his office became an Italian restaurant and Tommy held court. If the Dodgers lost, he still held court. Either way, if you hung out with Tommy you'd never go hungry.

On one Fan Appreciation Day, Tommy invited me into his office while the team was on the field during batting practice.

It was the last game of the season, and since the Dodgers were out of contention, it didn't mean anything.

"Don," said Tommy, "put on a uniform."

"Are you kidding?" I asked.

"No, I'm not kidding. You always wanted to be a Dodger. Well, here's your chance, buddy. We're about the same size, and I've got an extra. Go ahead, put it on and sit next to me. You'll love watching the game from the dugout."

I did. I was like a little kid. I loved sitting next to the guys and getting the players' point of view. It was a real kick in the head.

In the sixth inning, the Dodger pitcher got shelled.

"Go take him out, Don."

"What!"

"You heard me, go give him the hook. Yank him out and give the bullpen the signal for the southpaw."

Why the hell not!

It was a fantasy come true. I trotted out to the mound.

"Sorry, fella," I told the pitcher, "you're through."

"You're not the manager," he shot back. "You're not even a coach. You can't pull me out of the game."

"Give me the ball," I demanded.

"You're crazy," he said.

Meanwhile, homeplate umpire Harry Wendelstedt, a great veteran, headed out to the mound.

"What's going on here?" he asked.

When he got in my face, he saw who it was and said, "I'll be damned! Don Rickles! Don, any chance of getting me two tickets to see Dean Martin in Vegas?"

FOREVER FRIENDS

~~~~

One of the biggest honors of my life was when Frank Sinatra asked me to open for him during his final concert tours in the mid-nineties.

By then, I had long established a policy not to open for anyone. For Frank, though, I not only broke my policy, but I did so gratefully. I knew this was going to be show-business history. Touring with Sinatra—along with Frank, Jr., who was leading the orchestra—was something I wouldn't miss for the world.

By then, Frank was starting to have problems. But that doesn't mean he had lost his charm or his ability to thrill his fans. He had that until the end.

"Anything you particularly want me to do with my opening routine?" I asked him.

"Hey, Rickles," he said, "just enjoy yourself."

"Great," I said.

"Frank begged me to open for him," I announced as soon as I hit the stage. "A real mercy mission."

Our last hurrah together.

Equal billing, but Frank got $2 billion more than me.

When Frank hit the stage, he invited me back on. We did a bit where I'd come out and give him a drink.

"Thanks, Don," he'd say. "What's up?"

"Well, Frank, your close friend Vinnie Gallamano got two in the head. And Salvatore Boomboz got hit by a truck."

Frank broke up. Then we drank, both of us saying, "*A salut'.*"

One night when I went out there, though, Frank's memory was playing tricks on him.

"What are you doing?" he asked.

"I'm here to bring you a drink, Frank."

"I've got a drink."

"Look, Frank," I said, going into the routine, "Sal Maganazzo got whacked by Vinnie Luccalazzi—"

"I don't care," said Frank.

"But Frank—"

"Leave."

Suddenly, I was covered with flop sweat.

"Do me a favor, Don. Get lost."

I hurried off the stage. The funny thing was that the audience thought it was funny. They howled. They were sure it was part of the act.

I wasn't sure what it was.

Before the show, my dressing room was filled with important, well-connected guys who wanted to say hello to Frank, but Frank's door was closed.

"What do you think, Don? Should we knock on his door?" they'd ask me.

"What do I know? Knock on the door," I said. "But I'm not knocking."

Before our New York opening, one of the guys came to my dressing room. He was a big man, and he was wearing a bright yellow suit. He looked like he'd just fallen into a tub of butter.

"Look, Don," he said. "I'm your biggest fan. And I'm Frank's biggest fan. But do me a favor, don't draw any attention to me. I like to play it low-key. These days I need to keep a low profile."

When I came on stage, I saw him seated—in the front row yet. With his yellow suit, who could miss him?

"Ladies and gentlemen," I said, "I've played everywhere. But this is the first time," I added, pointing to the man in the yellow suit, "that I've ever played before a two-hundred-fifty-pound parakeet."

The big guy laughed, so his boys joined in.

Lucky me. I got to keep breathing.

●   ●   ●

"Frank, Vinnie just got two shots in the head."

After the tour, Frank struggled.

I'd go and visit him. We'd sit and watch a little television. At times when I noticed that Frank had lost that twinkle in his eyes, I knew it was time for Rickles to try to make him laugh.

May 1998.

I'm sitting in the Church of the Good Shepherd in Beverly Hills. I'm a pallbearer at Frank's funeral.

I think back a hundred years ago when he first came to see me in Miami Beach. I think of his generosity, his crazy humor, his fierce loyalty. I hear his voice, the greatest singing voice in the history of singing, a voice loved by people the world over.

At the end of the service, I walk up and stand in front of his coffin.

A priest gently points out that I'm leaning on the coffin.

"Oh, that's okay, Father," I say. "Frank wouldn't mind. I leaned on him my whole life."

We laid him to rest that afternoon.

Now when I'm relaxing with an iPod in my ears, I love listening to Frank. Frank's not going anywhere. His talent is forever.

MEMO

~~~~~~

FROM: Don Rickles

TO: Larry King
Jay Leno
Dave Letterman
Regis Philbin

SUBJECT: Selling Book

Now that this book's almost finished, I have to think about promoting it. I wonder if any of you guys could help me out?

Jay Leno:

He's a wonderful man, especially if your car needs a lube job. If he invites you to dinner, it's cheeseburgers in his garage. Jokes aside, Jay has a magnificent car collection.

Jay also has a great marriage and a great wife, Mavis. They're very compatible. She likes to travel, he likes to stay home and spit-shine his Chevys.

Jay has a big heart. When Johnny Carson died, he invited me and Newhart on his show to give a tribute. We had many beautiful memories of our dear friend, and Jay provided us with a national audience to pay respects to his predecessor.

Thanks, Jay, now what about my book?

Dave Letterman:

Funny guy.

Extrovert onstage, introvert offstage. Offstage he hides behind a baseball cap. Once, he came to my dressing room in Vegas. My dear friends Steve Lawrence and Eydie Gorme dropped by to wish me well, giving me many kisses and big hugs. The big emotions got Dave so nervous he ran out in the hall and hid.

When I'd appear on his show, I'd always kid him, "Dave, why don't we ever have dinner together?"

He'd laugh it off.

One night, though, when the show ended, his producer said, "Meet Dave at '21.' "

When Barbara and I got to "21," the maitre d' greeted us and led us down a flight of stairs. We found ourselves in the wine cellar. Dave was there with his full staff and a beautifully festive table. It was a great evening.

Before leaving, I took Dave aside, thanked him and then asked, "What about my book?"

Regis Philbin:

For many years, people have asked me, "What's Regis' talent?"

For many years, I've answered, "He believes it's singing."

The TV host and his idol.

Seriously, though, Regis is terrific. We've been friends for nearly fifty years. The man can talk. He can sing. He can tell a joke. Mostly, though, he screams.

In the old days, we'd walk down Hollywood Boulevard and Regis would scream, "I've got Rickles here! Say hello to Rickles!"

Even today Regis still screams. When it comes to promoting Rickles, he's unrelenting.

Regis has never been shy in creating fans. He'd interrupt robbers during a bank holdup to ask, "Hey guys, do you ever catch me on television?"

We've worked together in theaters where Regis would come to my dressing room before the show like he was shot

King finally meets a world leader.

out of a canon. "We're going to knock 'em dead tonight, Don!" he'd scream. "They're going to love us!"

He got me so worked up I'd do my finish before I started.

But I love the guy. Everyone does.

Now, Regis, what about my book?

Larry King:

I already told you stories about King back in Miami when we were both getting started.

Over the years, of course, Larry has gotten famous and very influential.

Here's what I like about Larry:

He interviews the Prime Minister of England or the French ambassador to the United Nations. Serious people, serious questions. He's getting to the bottom of some world crisis, and he does it with pinpoint clarity and total confidence.

Then, an hour later, after the broadcast, he's a different guy. We go to a deli where he says, "Should I have the corned beef lean or the pastrami thin without the cole slaw?" The man has a nervous breakdown over what to order.

"If you can decide what to ask the President of the United States," I say, "why can't you decide between pumpernickel and rye?"

"Maybe I'm better off with a scooped-out bagel and no butter," says Larry. "And maybe a little cottage cheese. That can't hurt me, can it, Don?"

"Larry, stop planning on living forever. Everyone's going to end up in a big talk show in the sky. But in the meantime, while you're here, what about my book?"

Pop-Pop holds court with grandsons, Harrison and Ethan.

BARBARA AND DON GO RIDING OFF INTO THE SUNSET

Beautiful life.

Beautiful wife.

Beautiful children, Mindy and Larry.

Beautiful grandchildren, Ethan and Harrison, and son-in-law, Ed.

Beautiful career.

What more can a man ask for?

My Barbara just gave me a beautiful party for my eightieth birthday. Steve and Eydie showed up to sing us "More," the same song they sang at our wedding party back at the Elegante in Brooklyn. Jack Carter got up and said, "Old age is rough. I thought I'd be living on a golf course, but instead I'm living at Walgreens."

Old age does have its challenges. But I feel great. And fortunately I'm out there working clubs and casinos all over the country. And fortunately audiences are still laughing.

The lady I love.

Thank you, God.

And thank you, Barbara, for being by my side and loving me all these years.

It's Sunday afternoon.

"Barbara," I say, "let's take a ride to the beach."

"Good idea, sweetheart," she says.

We get in the car. I'm behind the wheel.

"Isn't it great, Barb," I say. "Forty-one years together and here we are riding into a magnificent sunset."

"Watch where you're going, Don."

"I'm watching."

"You missed that stop sign."

"I stopped at the stop sign."

"You didn't stop, you rolled past it."

"I stopped."

"You're in the wrong lane to make a left turn, Don."

"Barb, don't yell at me. I hear you."

"Well, you're not listening."

"Please, I am listening. I'm getting in the left lane."

"There's a car in the left lane," she says. "And you're about to hit it."

"Barbara, I'm not going to hit it. I see it," I say.

"What are you talking about? You're not wearing your glasses."

For the next twenty minutes, it's a war of words. But when we reach the beach, get out of the car and watch the sky melt into the ocean, the world is right.

Dad celebrates with his family, Barbara, Larry and Mindy.

We look into each other's eyes, and my Barbara says, "You did drive in the wrong lane."

Still, the birds are chirping.

Seagulls are dive-bombing into the waves.

And with all that's going on, I look to the sky and say, "Thanks, Boss, for the wonderful life."

ABOUT THE AUTHORS

DON RICKLES is one of America's comic legends. Over the past fifty years, he has appeared in major motion pictures and television shows of virtually every genre. He continues to perform in nightclubs and casinos throughout the country. Rickles lives in Los Angeles.

DAVID RITZ has collaborated with Ray Charles, Aretha Franklin, B.B. King, Marvin Gaye and Bon Jovi, among others, on their autobiographies. His novels include *Blue Note Under a Green Felt Hat*; his lyrics include "Sexual Healing." Ritz lives in Los Angeles.